Parents and children in Prison
Attachment, separation and loss

GW00496920

Edited by Elaine Arnold

London League Publications Ltd
on behalf of
Separation & Reunion Forum

Parents and children in Prison
Attachment, separation and loss.

© Each chapter is copyright to the contributor. Introduction ©
Doctor Elaine Arnold. Dear Santa © Alison Henderson

The moral right of the contributors to be identified as the authors
has been asserted.

Cover design © Stephen McCarthy.

This book is copyright under the Berne Convention. All rights are
reserved. It is sold subject to the condition that it shall not, by
way of trade or otherwise, be lent, resold, hired out or otherwise
circulated without the publisher's prior consent in any form of
binding or cover other than that in which it is published and
without a similar condition being imposed on the subsequent
purchaser.

A CIP catalogue record for this book is available from the British
Library.

First published in Great Britain in November 2012 by:
London League Publications Ltd,
P.O. Box 65784, London NW2 9NS
On behalf of the Separation & Reunion Forum
Room 3, 250 York Road, London, SW11 3SJ

ISBN:	978-1903659-66-3
Cover design by:	Stephen McCarthy Graphic Design 46, Clarence Road, London N15 5BB
Layout:	Peter Lush
Printed and bound by:	Catford Print Centre, Catford SE6 4PY

Introduction

The Separation and Reunion Forum, in collaboration with the London Metropolitan University, held its twelfth annual conference on 24 November 2011. The theme was 'Imprisonment of Parents and Children: Exploring Attachment Separation and Loss' was decided upon early in the year, prompted by the continuing concern among its members of the high incidence of crime committed by young people, and especially of young black men and boys and the intense media coverage of the high numbers of them involved in the criminal justice system. Moreover, it was clear from conversations with some of the younger members of the Forum and some students that their knowledge of the prison system was limited and the effects of imprisonment on families was not a subject about which they thought. The conference was therefore welcomed as providing an opportunity for raising the level of awareness especially among lay people, social work students and students of counselling or therapy.

The Conference Committee felt justified in its selection of the theme when during the period 6 to 10 August 2011, rioting, looting and arson in several London boroughs and other cities and towns across England took the country by surprise and caused consternation among people from every level of the society. A worrying and shocking feature of the disturbances was the involvement of the numbers of children and young people. Among the first 1,000 people arrested, 66 per cent of those who appeared in court were under 25 years old and it was thought that 17 per cent were aged between 11 and 17 and a small number over 30. (Smith 2011).

The reaction to the riots on the part of the Prime Minister was blaming absent fathers, family breakdown and poor school discipline and threatening a series of tough measures to fight crime. Geoffrey Pearson (2011) claims that that this reaction of panics about criminal behaviour had happened in earlier times. Perhaps more questions need to be asked: Why do these riots happen? What do the rioters try to achieve? Is prevention possible? Who should be involved in trying to prevent them?

There was a high level of political debate about the level of punishment that should be given to the young people, of the tough measures that would be introduced to fight crime, and whether families of those involved in rioting should be evicted from their homes. This seemed to ignore the findings of the analysis of the backgrounds of those suspected of involvement in the disturbances that 41 per cent lived in one of the top 10 per cent of the most deprived places in the country. (Smith 2011) The findings of The Institute of Policy Research were that in the majority of the worst affected areas there was higher youth unemployment and significantly higher child poverty than the national average and lower education attainment. (IPPR August 2011)

If there is any possibility of promoting change, helping offenders and especially younger ones from embarking on crime as a career, it would be well to apply the old adage, 'Prevention is better than cure.'

Jeremy Corbyn MP, who spoke at the conference, recognised that if serious steps are to be taken to prevent young people from entering the justice system, "There is a need to look at the factors in the society which are at the root of the disaffection among young people which often lead them to crime."

When the young people were remanded into prison, in 2011, for those who had no previous convictions and who knew nothing of the conditions of life in prison, it was a traumatising experience. (Conversation with a voluntary worker)

Fortunately, within society there are a number of organisations the aims of which are to support the families and prisoners to cope with the trauma of separation and loss through imprisonment. They also help in rehabilitation with the aim of breaking the chain of offending and which sometimes can be transmitted intergenerationally.

Some of these organisations participated in the conference and gave delegates an insight into their work. Not only are they concerned about the individual's behaviour but some of them seek to influence policy toward providing more opportunities for rehabilitative services for offenders. Nevertheless it is necessary to consider the social context in which individuals behave. This is one of the principles advanced by the Forum since its inception as it focused on the work of John Bowlby who advocated the necessity of considering the environment in which the individual developed as well as his or her genetic potentials. (Bowlby 1988) There are instances where for some children a secure base was not experienced at home and they grew up with persistent feelings of insecurity, low self-esteem and poor educational attainment. They are likely to become dependent on peer groups to provide the sense of belonging. Unfortunately, some of these groups provide the opportunities for learning and practicing deviant behaviour.

My experience with young children who are labelled as being 'beyond their parents' control' has been that they are yearning for love and understanding of their attachment needs. Sometimes the parents themselves have been deprived of the opportunity to form secure emotional bonds in their early childhood and are unable to nurture their children. They see the deviance as the children's fault and often seek their removal, hoping that other carers would be able to change them. For some children there are positive outcomes when they are fostered or cared for in homes where the carers are themselves secure emotionally, understand the needs of the children and in their training the fundamental principles of attachment are taught and are understood. If no therapeutic help is given many of these children progress into secure custodial settings. An unsettling statistic is that "75 per cent of young people in custody have lived with someone other than their parent." (Lorraine Khan 2011)

The aim of the Conference, as with previous SRF conferences, was the raising of participants' awareness of the emotional needs of prisoners and their families; to highlight the importance of the understanding and utilisation of attachment theory in the assessments of offenders and to make recommendations of what needs to be done to help in the reduction of crime and to keep prisoners from reoffending.

The audience of 150 people included social workers, residential home staff, members of Youth Offending Teams, a rehabilitated offender, adoption and fostering agency staff, therapists, counsellors, doctors, teachers, mangers of voluntary agencies, day nursery staff and social work students from London Metropolitan University and Intercultural Therapy courses at Lambeth College.

The Conference Committee was pleased that the range of speakers had an abundance of knowledge, but also had experience of working therapeutically with prisoners and their families. They provided the audience with fascinating and inspiring presentations which prompted lively and stimulating debate and raised a range of emotions. Some expressed the desire to become involved in campaigns which could result in political solutions to remove the poor conditions which contribute to some of the causes of crime.

The conference was chaired by Alex Pascall OBE, who with his vast experience of radio broadcasting, meeting with groups in schools and in the community was a dynamic force in holding the conference together. He began by setting the scene of how keenly children feel the absence of a parent when separated by imprisonment. He had discovered a poem about a 12 year old girl writing to her mother at Christmas and asked Gerry German, the well-known champion of children excluded from school and an associate of the Separation and Reunion Forum to read to the audience. Alex, with brief anecdotes and gentle humour, helped to prevent the participants from being overwhelmed by the serious and intense subject matter.

The opening speaker of the conference was Rachel Wingfield, a psychotherapist and former chair of the Bowlby Centre, who possesses a vast knowledge of attachment theory and experience in clinical work with violent offenders in prison settings. She and Joseph Schwartz, also of the Bowlby Centre, were engaged in the My Story project, initiated by Roger Grimshaw, director of Research of the Centre for Crime and Justice. Rachel began by quoting Ezra Miller, an actor in the film *We need to talk about Kevin*, adapted from the book. He said "people were entitled to nothing in the world except for the one initial thing, the one intrinsic thing for healthy human development, the love of a mother or guardian." She recalled the importance of the early research of Dr John Bowlby whose seminal paper *44 Juvenile thieves* (1944) gave insights into the causes of crime. She drew attention to the report in the *Daily Telegraph* (November 2011) which described the My Story Project as groundbreaking and recommended it as required reading for a Home Secretary. She thought that the coverage was a hopeful sign of recognition that young people who commit crimes are human, as are their families.

Roger Grimshaw described the My Story Project. This was carried out as a partnership between the Centre for Crime and justice Studies and the Bowlby Centre. The project, through listening to the young people involved, was able to make the link of trauma with violence. The project demonstrated how narrative method can be used as a tool of understanding and engagement in response to violence shown by young offenders. It also indicated how well constructed service could provide preventative benefits.

Cherecee Williams, from Kinship Care and Imprisonment, outlined the benefits of kinship care for children whose mothers are imprisoned. She gave insight into the important role played as carers, especially by grandparents and other extended family members, and of some of the problems they encounter. She writes passionately about the need for more resources to facilitate this service in reaching its ultimate goal to ensure better outcomes for children.

Jim Rose, on 'How nurture protects children', spoke with conviction of the relevance of the core ideas of attachment theory when considering the impact a custodial sentence has on the relationship between parent and child. He highlighted the heated debates which have ensued when prison reformers have drawn attention to the plight of women in prison who self-harm, and who suffer the severe emotional pain of separation from their children. He stressed that relationship-based practices drawing upon the ideas of attachment theory provide most successful outcomes for parents and children.

Pamela Stewart's presentation, 'Molly and Child', was described by a participant as "heart-breaking". It highlighted how conditions of our childhood have long and far-reaching adverse effects on adult life if not modified by therapy.

The story of a woman with the ancestral history of slavery prompted a look at the long reach of slavery and the negative psychological effects on generations. The young woman had suffered severe trauma in her early life, but had committed the crime to avenge her sister who was being bullied at school. Pamela believed that therapy had helped to unlock meaning of her violent act to her client who had not divulged the awful things which had happened to her in her early life and her feelings about the absence of protection by her mother or surrogate carer.

In another moving presentation, a mother told her story of the experience of having her son imprisoned. She explained to the audience that she wanted them to have direct experience of him by showing the contents of his art portfolio. There were exquisite pencil drawings and pencil sketches and were displayed in the room. Some of his work had previously been displayed in the Mary Ward Centre. She spoke of her shock, disbelief and grief and that of the entire family when her son was involved in an incident which led to a fatal wounding with a weapon. Her son was a young man who did not express his feelings easily and had suffered an accumulation of losses through separation of parents and death of several family members. She pointed out that the accumulated losses impacted in unknown ways. She shared with the audience her feelings of being on trial as a mother. She was relieved that her son has been helped through a positive counselling relationship with the prison chaplain.

It was fitting that the last presentation of the day was entitled 'Breaking the Chain', because one of the aims of the conference was to promote ides of action to bring about a diminishing of crime, especially among young people.

Richard Uglow clearly described the programme 'Growth Journey' which has been delivered in male prisons for the past three years and which has had favourable outcomes. He stressed that criminal behaviour is always symptomatic of something deeper and helping individuals to find 'new resources' within themselves rather than stopping external behaviours is the key to rehabilitation of offenders. He focussed on separation 'inside' a person during the early years because of the environment, can, in the extreme, lead to criminal behaviour.

The workshop facilitators could all have been keynote speakers with the wealth of material they produced and participants wanted more time to engage with the issues. The workshops were: Lucy Keenan and Chrissie Wild: The offenders' journey: from arrest to release; Paul Rhys Taylor and Emmanuel King (Mentor, Prison Outreach Network): The role of religious groups in supporting prisoners and their families; Avril Johnson (Specialist Psychotherapeutic Therapist): The trauma of separation – a counsellor's Perspective; and Demetris Hapeshi and Anthony Sobers (London Metropolitan University): Precursors to problems of attachment for young people prior to imprisonment.

Gillian Paul, the chair of Separation and Reunion Forum, facilitated the panel discussion which concluded the conference. There were many comments and questions and a call for participants to disseminate the information and insights they had acquired among families, friends and colleagues. People were also encouraged to be aware of initiatives which might be aimed at policy makers to initiate preventative measures to help reduce crime. Participants expressed their appreciation of the efforts the conference made to organise a stimulating and informative event. Many were looking forward to the 2012 conference.

Elaine Arnold

Elaine Arnold is the Honorary Director of SRF. Her book, *Working with Families of African-Caribbean Origin: Understanding Issues around Immigration and Attachment* (Jessica Kingsley, 2012) can be ordered from any good bookshop.

References:

Bowlby, J. (1944) *Forty-four Juvenile Thieves: their characters and home life* International journal of Psychoanalysis 25 19-52: 107-127

Bowlby, J. (1988) *A Secure Base: Clinical Applications of attachment theory* Routledge, London

IPPR (2011) *The Institute of Policy Research Analysis* London

Khan, L. (2011) *An Alternative Route* in *Young Minds* magazine issue 114 Winter 2011/12 pp 26–27 London

Pearson, G. (2011) *Hooligan: a history of respectable fears* London, McMillan

Shriver, Lionel (2003) *We need to talk about Kevin* Serpent's Tail London

Smith, M. K. (2011) *Young people and the 2011 riots in England; experiences, explanations and implications for youth work* Paper presented at Seminar, Royal Festival Hall, 19 October 2011,The Rank Foundation Network

Acknowledgements

The Conference committee extends thanks for the donation from an anonymous donor which facilitated the successful administration and organisation of the conference and to all those who gave their time to participate as keynote speakers and workshop leaders and participants, volunteers and bookstall holders. SRF would like to thank the Conference chair, Alex Pascall, for his work for the event.

SRF would like to thank Training Link and Peter Lush for their support in producing this book, Stephen McCarthy for designing the cover and the staff of Catford Print Centre for printing it.

About the contributors

Dr Roger Grimshaw FRSA
(M.A. Cantab.; PhD Birmingham University)
Roger has been responsible for a range of research on criminology and social welfare over many years. With Rose Smith he was involved in a study of poverty and disadvantage in prisoners' families funded by the Joseph Rowntree Foundation. He led the team that evaluated the First Night in Custody scheme at HMP Holloway. Other work has looked at the information about imprisonment available to prisoners' families. Having spent much of his career at the National Children's Bureau, he is interested in how criminal justice impacts on families and children.

Rachel Wingfield Schwartz
Rachel Wingfield Schwartz (B.A., M.A. Cantab) is a UKCP Registered Psychotherapist and is the Clinical Director of the Clinic for Dissociative Studies. She was formerly the Chair of The Bowlby Centre for 8 years, where she is also a training supervisor and lecturer. Rachel has a wide range of clinical experience in a variety of settings including forensic settings, and has specialised in working with survivors of trauma and abuse, including sexual abuse, rape, domestic violence, war, state terror, torture and organised abuse. She has undertaken clinical work with offenders, including violent offenders, in prison and other therapeutic settings. Rachel has a particular interest in concepts of diagnostic labelling, 'unsuitability' and 'untreatability' in relation to psychotherapy and how they are used to distance us from working towards change with traumatised or violent people. Rachel is currently a Consultant for the Centre for Crime and Justice Studies.

Cherecee Williams
Cherecee Williams's involvement in the criminal justice system and the voluntary sector began in 2001 as a Family Support Volunteer for the Prison Advice and Care Trust. Her role was to provide information, advice and support to those affected by imprisonment.
Over the years she has maintained the focus of supporting prisoners and their families by carrying out a number of roles. These roles included the assistant manager for the Holloway Prison Visitors' Centre with a focus on volunteer coordination, Volunteer/Mentor Coordinator of the Exodus project which helped offenders and ex-offenders through the resettlement phase.
Her current role is the Kinship Care Support Service Manager, supporting friends and family carers looking after the children of prisoners in HMP Holloway.

Jim Rose

Jim has a long career in work with children and young people mainly in residential settings, including the management of secure accommodation. From 1998 to 2001 he was the professional advisor to the Home Office on the placement and management of young people sentenced to long term custody for serious offences.

From January 2004 to December 2008 Jim was the director of The Nurture Group Network, a national charity with the aims of promoting and supporting nurture groups in schools and encouraging the development of nurturing approaches to work with children and young people in all settings.

As well as being a trustee of the Caspari Foundation, Jim is a director of an independent fostering agency. He has written two books, *Working with Young People in Secure Accommodation – From Chaos to Culture,* and the recently published, *How Nurture Protects Children.*

Pamela Stewart

Pamela was born in Texas and moved with parents to Europe in 1963. She studied History of Art, and as a result of birth of her children became interested in early development and teaching. She received an MA distinction at the Tavistock in 1998. Her dissertation was *Born Inside* –– an observation of mothers and babies in HMP Holloway. She does ongoing work in HMP Holloway, Bronzefield, Feltham and Wormwood Scrubs, and also works in private practice and as a supervisor.

Richard Uglow

Richard is founder and managing director of Enrichyou, a company that enables the growth of people at all levels of life. Set up in 2000, Richard has developed an accredited programme called 'The Growth Journey' which unlocks the essence of a person in all of life's settings. He has delivered the Growth Journey in prisons, schools, churches, family settings and in businesses. It can be used in a restorative and therapeutic context or in a formative and proactive development approach. The programme works with the whole person – to assist people to find peace and fulfilment. Due to lack of understanding, lack of political vision and the economic climate the programme is only run on a private basis at the moment – although it is fully accredited by the Her Majesties Prison Service.

The majority of Richard's work is in the workplace where he develops leaders to work from 'wholeness and integrity' and assists directors to run sustainable businesses.

Richard is a qualified professional coach, a master practitioner in NLP, a qualified accountant and former finance director and a former Territorial Army officer. He is married with two children, and lives in Lincolnshire.

Lucy Keenan

Lucy Keenan is the development director at Action for Prisoners' Families where she manages a small team whose work includes delivering awareness raising training and engaging with local services to recognise the issues facing the children and families of offenders. Lucy joined APF in 2002 to co-ordinate the Prisoners' Families helpline. Prior to this, Lucy spent eight years with the crime reduction charity NACRO where she had a number of roles including working as an information officer and then develop-ping the Resettlement Information Service.

Chrissie Wild

Chrissie Wild joined Prisoners' Families and Friends Service in April 2011. As Befriending Services Manager she recruits, trains, deploys and supervises volunteers to act as befrienders to the families and friends of anyone sentenced to imprisonment or remanded in custody. Prior to her present role, Chrissie was project manager of the SOVA Young People's Support Project in the London Borough of Bexley for 10 years.

Demetris Hapeshi

Demetris joined the London Metropolitan University in 1998 from the University of Salford where he was course leader for the BSc (Hons) Social Policy and BSc (Joint Hons) Health Science and Social Policy. He also taught extensively on the Salford's DipSW and MA Dip SW Programmes. Before then Demetris taught on Mid-Kent College's Dip SW and was Principal Training Officer (Child Care and Child Protection) for the London Borough of Southwark. Demetris has practiced in Hackney (as a residential social worker), Wandsworth (as both a generic and children and families social worker) and has managed a residential establishment in Greenwich. He has also undertaken extensive freelance training for a variety of organisations including the Family Rights Group. Demetris is the MSc course leader at London Metropolitan University. His main teaching areas are Social & Theoretical Perspectives in Social Work, Assessment & Ethics and Law. Demetris is currently undertaking research into whether social workers and social work students perceive any contradiction between their or their colleague's religious beliefs and their responsibilities as social workers.

Anthony Sobers

Anthony has a BA (Hons), Postgraduate Diploma in Applied Social Studies, CQSW, RMN, SRN, Diploma in Training and Certificate in Counselling.
He joined London Metropolitan University in 1987 after practising as a training officer in Social Services with a specific brief in the areas of fostering & adoption, mental health, student training and development,

Anti-discriminatory perspectives, post qualifying courses for social workers and managers. He has experience as a consultant and counselling supervisor for Barnardo's, and other teaching organisations and for a voluntary agency for people with HIV / AIDS. His main teaching experience is centred on mental health, psychotherapeutic group work and counselling perspectives, work with children & families, management of change in organisations and social research for social workers. Research interests include: The development of new perspectives in intercultural psychotherapy and counselling; the attributes of the communication and psychotherapeutic processes in HIV/ AIDS.

Paul Rhys-Taylor

Paul is a husband and a father, a social worker and a practice teacher. Since 1993, he has been a volunteer prison visitor for the Prison Outreach Network (PON), an exciting inter-church ministry to prisons in the UK. Paul fronts a band that performs in prisons across the South East of England and on the Isle of Wight. The message in the music is one of hope and after each gig, Paul gets to spend individual time with the inmates, offering them support and encouragement.

Since 1997, Paul has managed an independent sector residential care service for boys aged 11 to 18 in public care. His prison work with adult men fuels his drive to promote outcomes that divert the boys in his care away from offending and future incarceration.

Emmanuel King

Emmanuel is a husband and a father; and since 1989, he has been the director of the Prison Outreach Network (PON), a dynamic inter-church ministry to prisons in the UK. The Prison Outreach Network operates under the umbrella of the Global Outreach Network, which is a registered charity.

Emmanuel's longstanding pastoral dedication and leadership of a network of volunteer prison visitors led to an appointment in the Prison Service in 2008. Since then, Emmanuel has worked as a Chaplain both at Rochester and Isis Young Offenders Institutions (HMYOI) and at (HMP) Brixton Prison, where he has had substantial contact with incarcerated men of all ages. Emmanuel's passion and work with male offenders has always been around maximising manhood.

Separation & Reunion Forum

The Separation and Reunion Forum (SRF) emerged following a meeting, between Dr Elaine Arnold, and a small group of women of African-Caribbean origin in 1999. They had been interviewed about separation during their early years from their parents and the subsequent reunion.

The women recalled their experiences of the pain of parental loss, as well as the loving care received from their grandmothers and other members of the extended families. They remembered their confusion when they were reunited in the UK with parents who were strangers to them, younger siblings and the strangeness of the new country. Also discussed were difficulties they experienced – at home, school and in the wider community.

The group wanted to raise awareness of the long lasting traumatic effects on the emotional wellbeing of children and families who had experienced broken attachments, separation and loss in their early years. **SRF's** first conference was held in 2000. It was felt that lessons from the past century could inform the future.

SRF stresses that the significant long-lasting adverse effects of separation and loss arise not just from immigration, but are present in adoption, fostering, long period of hospitalisation, boarding school, and imprisonment & death of family members & close friends.

SRF bases its work on the principles of Attachment Theory. It is now in the process of changing its name to Supporting Relationships and Families.

SRF has held conferences in collaboration with Goldsmiths College, the Caspari Foundation and for the past eight years the London Metropolitan University's faculty of Social Science and Humanities.

SRF runs bi-monthly workshops on topical issues as well as its annual conference, and offers training on Attachment Theory. For more information, visit www.serefo.org.uk

Contact details: Room 3, 250 York Road, London SW11 3SJ
Tel: 020-7801-0135; email: serefo.info@gmail.com

Charity no. 1132487

Contents

Prison Poem by Alison Henderson

A girl writes a letter to Santa asking him to get her mom released from prison.

Dear Santa

Me and Mum would always write
dear Santa Claus a note,
but this year Mum won't be around
so this is what I wrote:

Dear Santa if I had one wish
to make all on my own,
it would be to release my Mum
and let her please come home.

Grandma makes the Christmas roast
with lots of food to eat,
but this year in the dining room
there'll be an empty seat.

I know it's far too much to ask
so this year there's no wish,
but Santa could I ask you to
deliver my Mum this...

Trust me Mum you will get through
don't cry or shed a tear,
we'll celebrate our Christmas day
when you come home next year.

You told us to enjoy ourselves
but I can't promise that,
I'll miss you telling Christmas jokes
wearing your party hat.

I love you Mum with all my heart
be strong and please don't cry,
Christmas day will come and go
and time will soon fly by.

I know you made a big mistake
but what is done is done,
prison's stole our Christmas but...
they'll never steal my Mum.

To Mum with love.

Dedicated to Sandra currently serving five years in prison in the UK.
With thanks to Alex Pascall and Alison Henderson. This poem was read to the
conference by Gerry German, who sadly died earlier this year.

1. My story
Young people talk about the trauma and violence in their lives: Why does it matter?

Roger Grimshaw

Trauma, separation and criminal justice

Criminal justice is no stranger to trauma and through the institution of prison exacts its own toll. Imprisonment is rising, bringing with it greater pains of separation. Official figures show that the actual population stood at 87,573 by the end of October 2011. Projections meanwhile indicated the likelihood of further increases, the forecasts lying in a range from 83,100 to 94,800 by the end of June 2017. [1]

Action for Prisoners' Families, a charity supporting work with families, has estimated that 160,000 children experience separation as a result of imprisonment and that 17,700 of these were children separated from their mothers.[2] For many young people in prison, trauma is not new; it is something they experience before they cross the threshold. The exceptional level of trauma commonly experienced by young people in juvenile justice is only slowly being recognised.

"Research shows that while up to 34 per cent of children in the United States have experienced at least one traumatic

---

[1] Ministry of Justice 2011
[2] APF, 2011

event, between 75 and 93 per cent of youth entering the juvenile justice system annually in this country are estimated to have experienced some degree of trauma." [3]

A recent literature review noted studies showing that 33 per cent to 92 per cent of children in custody have experiences of some form of maltreatment, while in one study over 50 per cent of those who committed violent offences experienced traumatic separation. [4]

There is growing policy interest in the violent and traumatic backgrounds experienced by many young people convicted of serious violent acts. A report from the Children's Commission for England commenting on young prisoners stated that "the majority of children who commit offences have awful histories of abuse, abandonment and bereavement." [5] The cross-government report on gang and youth violence published in November 2011 observed that risk factors such as parental neglect and violence recur time and again" in the childhoods of young people who commit violent acts. [6]

A different perspective

While criminal justice focuses on a harmful event, which can be certainly horrific when scrutinised in court, we asked if it

---

[3] Adams, 2010 p. 1

[4] Day et al 2008, p. 6 and p. 28

[5] Office of the Children's Commissioner, 2011,p 5

[6] Home Office 2011, p. 10

might be possible to uncover trauma in the childhoods of young people convicted of grave crimes- kidnapping, rape or murder. By articulating experiences for themselves, young people could bear witness to whole sequences of previous events which were equally disturbing and would go a long way to explaining the emotional basis for their involvement in violence. It was the potential for revealing the emotional history of children which underpinned the participation of psychotherapists in the project. They could bring an interpretative framework which was sensitive to the implications of the young people's narratives for a deeper understanding of the links between childhood trauma and subsequent violence.

The project therefore juxtaposed three kinds of narrative: the event witnessed in court and analysed by criminal justice; the child's account of a difficult childhood; and the history unearthed by the therapist which is normally developed under clinical conditions.

Designing a narrative-based project

The considerations animating the project meant that the stories had to be facilitated in a process of co-production which was sensitive to the needs of the young people and respected their right to own their stories. They were to hold the copyrights to the individual stories. A joint team with social research and psychotherapeutic experience was formed in order to undertake the research and to monitor the well-being of the participants. Young people serving prison sentences were to be interviewed and their words recorded so that the spontaneity of their narratives could be preserved. At each stage the team reviewed the process and examined the stories as they emerged in order to guide the project through to completion. In all research projects it is important to ensure the confidentiality and anonymity of the subjects; in this one, given the media interest in 'child monsters', it was paramount to ensure the safety of the participants by maintaining strict control over the information associated with the work, so that they were not vulnerable to the adverse effects of revelations. The interests of victims' families were also significant in recognising the sensitive nature of the authorship. Finally the storytellers were given the option to receive personal support once the accounts had been published.[7]

Partnerships

The project was conducted as a partnership between the Centre for Crime and Justice Studies and the Bowlby Centre, and supported by the Paul Hamlyn Foundation. The research obtained ethics committee approval at King's College London and a proposal to undertake it was accepted by the NOMS Research Committee.

---

[7] Grimshaw et al, eds. 2011

It was then a matter of approaching prison governors and working closely with staff in the prisons. A distinguished group of advisors gave generous guidance. Without the support of all these partners it would have been impossible to produce the stories in the form that had been envisaged.

The selection of participants

All the young people eligible to take part would have been convicted of a 'grave crime' under the Powers of Criminal Courts (Sentencing) Act 2000 and were expected to be adults placed in young offender institutions. Once access had been made to the young offender institutions, staff were asked to nominate possible participants who were invited to discuss the project and their informed consent was sought. Using file information it was intended that individuals with mental health and other conditions affecting memory would be excluded.

Process

The stories were generated using biographical narrative interview methods.[8] The simple request for the individual to 'tell a story' is the starting point and the repetition of the request as one story closes means that another one follows and so on. In practice the young people displayed an evident narrative urgency despite some lapses of memory.

---

[8] Wengraf 2001

At points where traumatic events were recounted it was important to acknowledge their expression by a process of positive listening. Each recorded interview was transcribed and discussed among the team; if need be support was offered to the young person. It took a series of sessions for the stories to be concluded.

The raw interview texts were inevitably rough-edged so they were edited, removing names, repetition and half-statements, as well as the facilitator's questions and responses. The edited texts were then taken back to young people for approval and agreements to publish were then signed by the three authors.

Linking trauma and violence

The offences of the two men and one woman included murder, rape and false imprisonment, for which their imprisonment terms ranged from four years to life. Equally they had been victims of trauma, through bereavement, interruption of care and abuse.

The introduction to the publication explains how John Bowlby's ideas about 'attachment' help to identify links between childhood relationships with primary carers and subsequent violence. Inconsistency or rejection by parental figures leads to anger and insecurity. Damage to the child's model of the external world creates the potential for violence in response to frustration.[9]

---

[9] De Zulueta, 2006; Boswell , 1995

6

Implications

The implications of the project highlight how narrative methods can be tools of understanding and engagement in responding to violence shown by young people. The findings indicate once again how well-constructed supportive services for children and families could have preventative benefits. Once the roots of violence are better understood, young people like the authors of the stories can be seen in a new light as candidates for therapeutic assessment, diagnosis, and treatment. Services which promote long term recovery become vital parts of the management of young people's needs.

In terms of policy the stories suggest that the attribution of criminal responsibility and the imposition of a sentencing tariff hardly begin to appreciate the individual's state of mind and personal development. A modern approach to young people's violent actions requires attention to the central role of past trauma, and implies a very different kind of thinking about responsibility, one which asserts that recovery is the road to taking responsibility for one's actions. The stories can assist advocates and campaigners who wish to challenge stereotypes of young people's involvement in violence. Leaders of coordinated children's services can use the stories as discussion material for planning exercises and for illustration within training courses.

Responding to the trauma which underlies young people's violence means intervening in different places and at different levels. Services for young people in custody should be prepared to offer treatment and support. Any indication that senior staff in young offender institutions acknowledge the importance of attachment must be welcomed.[10] Young people displaying symptoms of trauma in the community need tailored casework, while services dealing with domestic violence and protecting children should be ready to facilitate the long term support that will address the insidious effects of trauma, over a period of years if necessary.

We believe it is crucial that these stories make an impact, not just by themselves, but in making it possible for others in the fields of practice and policy to be alert to the potential stories that young people have to tell.

References

Action for Prisoners' Families (2011) *"Children of incarcerated parents" Submission to the Committee on the Rights of the Child, Day of General Discussion*. Geneva, Switzerland, Office of The High Commissioner For Human Rights
www2.ohchr.org/english/bodies/.../ActionforPrisonersFamilies.doc
Adams, E. (2010) *Healing invisible wounds: Why Investing in Trauma-Informed Care for Children Makes Sense* Washington DC, Justice Policy Institute
Boswell, G. (1995) *Violent victims: the prevalence of abuse and loss in the lives of Section 53 offenders* London, The Prince's Trust.

---

[10] Office of the Children's Commissioner 2011, p.37

De Zulueta, F. (2006) *From Pain to Violence. The traumatic roots of destructiveness* Chichester, John Wiley.

Grimshaw, R., with Schwartz, J., and Wingfield, R. eds. (2011), *My Story: young people talk about the trauma and violence in their lives,* London: Centre for Crime and Justice Studies http://www.crimeandjustice.org.uk/mystorystructure.html

Home Office (2011) *Ending Gang and Youth Violence: A Cross-Government Report* Cm 8211

Ministry of Justice (2011) *Prison Population Projections 2011 – 2017 England and Wales* Ministry of Justice Statistics Bulletin www.justice.gov.uk/downloads/publications/statistics-and-data/mojstats/prison-pop-projections-2011-17.pdf

Office of the Children's Commissioner (2011) *'I think I must have been born bad' Emotional wellbeing and mental health of children and young people in the youth justice system* London, Office of the Children's Commissioner www.rcpch.ac.uk/sites/default/files/I_think_I_must_have_been_born_bad_-_full_report%20%281%29.pdf

Day, C., Hibbert, P., and Cadman, S. (2008) *A Literature Review into Children Abused and/or Neglected Prior Custody* London, Youth Justice Board www.yjb.gov.uk/publications/Resources/Downloads/Abused%20prior%20to%20custody.pdf

Wengraf, T. (2001) *Qualitative research interviewing; biographic narrative and semi-structured methods* London, Sage

2. My Story
Three young people in prison talk about their lives.

Rachel Wingfield Schwartz

As a psychotherapist with experience of working with young people in prison, I was asked to become a consultant on this project with the Centre for Crime and Justice Studies, and it has been a privilege to be involved with it. As members of the Separation and Reunion Forum, concerned with issues of family break up, trauma, separation and loss, I don't need to tell you how central these issues are to any understanding of violent crime; and to the lives of young people and families who end up in the prison system.

Last week, the *Daily Telegraph* ran a piece about the My Story research, describing it as a "groundbreaking new report", which "reveals the truth about how our society fails its violent young". It also concluded that the report should be "required reading for any Home Secretary". This kind of coverage, from a traditionally right wing newspaper, may be a hopeful sign, that finally society is beginning to accept that young people who commit violent crimes, including those in prison, are human beings, as are their families.

Much of the time, our society portrays children and teenagers convicted of violence, as evil monsters who we should simply lock up and throw away the key.

In a recent interview about his role in the film *We Need to talk about Kevin*, actor Ezra Miller describes himself as being 'haunted' by playing the role of a teenage boy who commits acts of violence and murder. He says he feels the film has a lot to say about "the anger of today's youth": "If an offspring is not given proper attention it just does whatever it has to, to get attention. People are entitled to nothing in the world except for the one initial thing, the one thing that is so intrinsic for human development – the love of a mother or guardian."

The young people's stories in this report reveal that what lies behind the violent and grave crimes they committed, is a lot more complex than needing attention, and more extreme and more violent, than simply lacking the love of a mother or guardian. Nonetheless, Ezra Miller makes a crucial point here. As early as 1944, in his groundbreaking work *44 Juvenile Thieves* researcher and psychoanalyst John Bowlby established the link between what he then termed 'maternal deprivation' and criminal behaviour in children. We now understand 'maternal deprivation' to mean more generally, the abandonment, separation or loss experienced by a child in relation to its caregivers. The Separation and Reunion Forum has long drawn on Bowlby's work, to highlight the impact of broken attachment on intergenerational transmission of trauma and violence in families and communities.

Researchers since Bowlby have continued to establish this link between deprivation of care, a lack of a secure base with reliable attachment figures, and crimes of violence committed by young people. Long periods of separation, multiple changes in caregivers, and loss of attachment figures are all significant in the histories of violent young offenders, including the three interviewees you will read about here. Currently, one third of young people in prison grew up in the care system. One of our three young interviewees also spent most of his life in care. As Bowlby put it: "Nothing substitutes for a secure base."

In addition to deprivation of care, the My Story Project demonstrates that the narratives of young people who end up committing grave violent crimes, also include severe, multiple and prolonged forms of trauma; these additional traumas are key in enabling us to understand the roots of their crimes. By the time of their index offence, these children and teenagers had themselves had many serious violent crimes committed against them. One interviewee also witnessed repeated domestic violence against her mother by her father. We know that young people who have suffered from painful abandonment and loss, often go on to re-enact their painful experiences; this can result in their committing violent acts that harm themselves and others.

One of our interviewees experienced neglect and abandonment by both parents, as well as physical and sexual abuse. The only times his father did promise to visit him, including on his birthdays, he did not show up. Frequently with abandonment trauma comes feelings of "I am not worth much" which produces repetitions of self-sabotage, of ruining good things because they are not felt to be deserved. One of our interviews shows this form of repetition.

"One minute I can be okay and then a minute later, I can start to kick off, I can just change in seconds and my whole attitude, my whole mentality. I'll be calm and then I'll just get angry and then I'll just think 'Fuck it, I've got nothing to work towards now, I've lost it all anyway, just go do what you've got to do'. I used to ruin things for myself, like, I would have something coming up like maybe a football match that I wanted to go to, or play for like the school, and I'd know that that's coming up and I'd do something to stop myself from being able to go. Not meaning to, but it would just happen, that I'd kick off and then they'd say 'No you can't go,' and then I'll get really upset about it. So everything that was going well for me I'd end up destroying it some way. That's just the way it was."

Whenever a serious injustice is committed against a child by his or her caretakers, there is implicitly a 'third party' involved in this abuse. Alongside perpetrator and victim, is society – the adults in the world around children and the institutions put in place to protect children. The role of the 'third party' can either be that of witness and rescuer of children from the danger they are in, or the third party can play the role of bystander and perhaps unintentional colluder in the continuing trauma and abandonment unfolding in a child's life.

Throughout these stories, the interviewees describe failed attempts by a range of services to intervene in the trauma they were experiencing. They describe even more

13

examples of points where opportunities for intervention were missed altogether by the different services involved in their lives: teachers, social workers, police, courts and the care system.

Each one of these young people was exhibiting well-known signals of severe distress in the years leading to their offence, and these symptoms escalated in the months immediately prior to the offence. Two interviewees describe the loss of their father as a turning point in their 'going off the rails' shortly before their offences; one interviewee describes the traumatic loss of his father, when his father was sent to prison: "'My mum phoned the police and said 'Oh, I've been kicked out the house' by my dad, and my dad was on bail at the time. Basically, by doing that, my dad would go to prison because he didn't have a bail address. So I remember there was like six or seven of the big police wagons there was the little cars there was a good 50, 60 police officers there just trying to remove my dad and his friend from the house. But they didn't go round the back, everyone was just stood out front. I remember looking out my bedroom window and... seeing the police everywhere and then my dad put some music on really loud and he packed his bags and he'd snuck me out the back door with his friend, and we got out the back gate and we walked round and got away from the police, but because he had me in his arms, he was using me to his advantage really, and he knew that the police weren't going to touch him, because he was physically carrying me. So basically we got to the end of the road and we got out of the estate ... But he knew he was going to get arrested at the same time so he just sat there. He explained things to me that he could be gone for a while. He knew that he'd lost the battle in a way. I remember him crying, which made me cry ... When we got to the end of the road, we sat there just waiting for my friend to pick me up, and then I realised that I wasn't going to see my dad for a while. I can't even remember how I realised but I remember I was terrified. I didn't want to lose my dad."

This is such a powerful expression of how deeply loss is experienced.

The two interviewees who lost their fathers were regularly in trouble with teachers and police during the period after the loss, and yet no-one around them was able to recognize or act on, these obvious signs of profound trauma and grief. Yet it has been demonstrated that (recent) loss is a key risk factor in grave childhood violence. These two young people went on to be involved in violent offences including murder and false imprisonment.

Another interviewee describes interventions from the age of 18 months, when social services put him on the child protection register. He was on the register as a result of suspicions he had been sexually abused by his father and was exhibiting sexualized behaviour. There had also been incidents in which his mother hung him over a balcony, threatening to drop him, and in which he was left alone wandering outside in the early hours of the morning. He was not removed from the home until the age of seven, by which time his attachment to his mother was very strong, and he had already been found sexually abusing another child. He was told he had to make a choice between going to a boarding school for children with behavioural difficulties, or of being fully removed from his mother's care, and not allowed to see her again until he was 16 years old.

At boarding school, he was involved in an incident in which he and others boys barricaded an 11 year old girl into her room and he says "took turns in having sex with her". When the staff finally broke into the room, they responded by only asking the boys if they would like to have a shower.

At 13, this boy went on to rape a little girl.

As you read these young people's stories, you will notice yourself how clear the signs were that something was wrong, and the places where intervention might have been possible.

As a psychotherapist, I would like to add that even if intervention does not happen earlier, there is still an enormous opportunity to bring about change for young people and their families, when a young person or parent is in prison. I know from experience that if a form of psychotherapy is put in place in prison, which enables broken and traumatic attachments to be understood and worked through, young people can leave prison far less likely to reoffend, and with a capacity to be loving parents themselves and responsible members of our community.

The young people we interviewed are aware that there is much to be learned from their stories, by themselves, by other young people in trouble, by services and perhaps

16

most of all, by parents. They are clear that they want to tell these stories, not because they want sympathy, but because they want to contribute to an understanding of how such grave crimes by young people happen.

One young interviewee gives us some moving advice on how we can respond to and learn from these stories: "I don't want people to read it and go 'Oh, I feel sorry for him'. I mean there's no need to, I'm perfectly fine. Everything's that's happened to me happened for a reason and it's made me the person I am today. So I want people to read it and say these are some of the reasons why I got in the situations that I got in because I thought everything was normal, and I didn't really understand a lot of things when I was young. So maybe, for example, a young parent reads this and then goes, 'Oh I'm a bit like his parents', and then they go, 'Well I don't want my kid going to jail, I don't want him to feel like how I felt as a kid, I don't want him going to jail when he's like 14, 15 for getting involved in a murder or something like that'. So that's where I'm coming from really."

References

Bowlby, J. (1944) *Forty-four Juvenile Thieves: their characters and home life. International journal of Psychoanalysis* 25 19-52: 107-127

Shriver, Lionel (2005) *We need to talk about Kevin* London, Serpent's Tail

3. Molly and child
Psychotherapeutic work with a young woman in prison

Pamela Stewart

How to convey emotional experience? Throughout history we have used stories to explain experiences to ourselves. Yet increasing psychotherapists are required to give evidence of our work – how can this be done? Our work is hard to categorize; statistics feel reductive, trivialisers of meaning. While I will offer statistics, first I would like to tell you a story about my work over 18 months with a young woman from the Caribbean.

To begin I will describe my psychotherapeutic work with Molly, first in a pregnancy group and then with her in a mother and baby unit. From this I will consider conclusions and finally relate them to statistics to see if any fuller understanding of her story can be gained when placed in the wider context of early experience and female offending and punishment in Britain in the 21st century.

Molly and I first met when she was several months pregnant and she chose to attend a weekly therapy group for pregnant women in prison. For the past 11 years I have facilitated a weekly group for pregnant women and a group for mothers and babies. The purpose of these two weekly groups is to provide a reflective, confidential setting. In this setting the women are encouraged to explore their feelings about becoming a mother. This exploration raises many issues.

One theme which frequently emerges is the woman's own sense of abandonment in her childhood. Being in touch with these sad feelings enables her to imagine a different kind of childhood for her soon to be born baby. If she is in prison long enough we then have the opportunity to work together in the mother and baby group. Here patterns of mothering from the past arise and can be experienced within the group. The goal for the mother and baby group is to encourage the mother's curiosity in her baby and to see the baby as a real person, not just an extension of herself.

On first meeting Molly I saw a very small young woman with bright eyes. Molly was 19 years old and had been sentenced for grievous bodily harm. In the confidential group the women do not always discuss their offence or their sentence. Sometimes these are not mentioned at all. Molly's attendance was very punctual and reliable. She was always waiting, unlike many of the more reluctant participants. One week, when all the attendees were from the Caribbean, the women started to talk about their childhoods. One of the pregnant women began by telling of a young girl who had lived next door to her at home in the island. She described the violence meted out to this young woman which resulted in her being gang-raped at the age of 14 and thrown down a well where she died. The pregnant women in the group then spoke for a long time about what it was like growing up in the Caribbean without the care of their parents who were away working in the UK. Molly said that her own mother had left her behind on the island. Molly's mother wanted to come to London and work in order to send money home to her own mother who was looking after Molly and her little sister. In hearing the women speak I had a very strong sense that the parents were not leaving their children behind thoughtlessly. The parents needed to leave in order to have the funds to care for the children. All around the world we see this pattern of mothers leaving their children in order to send money home to care for them. I doubt if this decision is pain-free for anyone.

The other women in the group joined in with their own experiences of being left behind, separated from parents who had gone abroad to earn money for a better life. They spoke of the strict discipline and the lack of education available to them, of missing their mothers and longing for the parcels they were sent irregularly from the UK. While the grandparents were presented as strict and authoritarian it also sounded as if the children ran unsupervised much of the time, apart from Sundays when they were expected to dress nicely and to attend church.

Molly said that she and her sister played outside a lot with very little adult supervision. Speaking longingly of the beautiful weather and the sunshine, Molly also spoke of a darker side. There were always lots of older boys hanging around which she found threatening. Molly was not imagining this threat. Jeered and taunted for days for wearing such skimpy clothes Molly was brutally raped by several boys one day. According to the boys this was to teach her a lesson about how to dress. Of course the problem with how to dress was not due to a lack of taste. Grinding poverty was the reason for the skimpy clothes. Ashamed and lonely, Molly told no one. Molly was 12 years old. Like many of the children around her Molly dreamed of the day that her mother would write to her and say that the time had come for Molly and her sister to join her in London. Molly had a long wait. Finally, when she was 14, she and her sister travelled alone to meet their mother, who by now was basically a stranger. It is not hard to imagine the disappointment she felt when she arrived in December from there to what she had imagined to be the 'Promised Land'. Not only was the weather horrible and strange, but her mother and father had split up, her father moving to another country. In his place were a new partner and two new, unsuspected siblings all living together in a very small flat in south London.

Molly's physical and emotional dislocation was compounded by an educational system beyond her grasp. In the pregnancy group Molly was a bright, articulate young woman. However, the large school with the many teachers, students and subjects was a chaotic nightmare full of signals she could not read. No one noticed as Molly drifted off and stopped attending regularly. Life was a little easier for her sister who was younger. Both girls missed their former island home, feeling homesick and disappointed that their dream of a reunion with their mother was so out of touch with the reality of life in London.

During the day Molly said that her house was deserted. The children were all meant to be at school and would come home and fend for themselves until the adults arrived around 7pm, tired and harassed from their own long working day. Molly was increasingly being bullied at school, with gangs of girls following her around and jeering at her clothes and the way she spoke. To avoid this she increasingly avoided school, withdrawing into herself, lost in her own sense of isolation. At times her hopes would rise. Talk of her father coming to visit London excited her. Plans would be made for her to go and meet him. Sadly these times ended with her sitting alone in MacDonald's for hours with no sign of her father or even a message to say he could not meet with her that day.

As her time in the group increased so did her willingness to continue her story. Being listened to seemed to increase her capacity for self-expression and Molly's insight and eloquence increased. Several months into the group, and by now heavily pregnant, Molly described her offence.

Molly left school and was able to find her way on a training course. The bullying had stopped for her but not for her younger sister. One afternoon after school the girls that had been bullying her sister showed up at their home. Breaking in with baseball bats they beat up Molly's sister. With no adults in the house no one was there to protect Molly and her sister, and neither considered calling the police. Mistrust of the police is a constant with these young women. The police are seen as racist and of such little use that the idea to ring them is never mentioned.

Devastated by her failure to protect her sister, Molly also linked to her own experience of being raped and unprotected back in the Caribbean. The idea that she could be angry that there were no responsible adults around to protect her was dismissed. What an idea? Where did I get the idea that there were benign authority figures around to protect her? At this point Molly was looking at me as if I was from Mars. I did ask her if she was wondering whether a white, more than middle-aged woman could understand her. Molly smiled and said, "Well, at least you turn up and try".

Again Molly felt that she had to take the world on her own shoulders. Alone. And where would she have been otherwise? Later, desperate for revenge, Molly managed to kidnap one of the girls, beat her up, strip her, put her in the boot of her mother's car and drive to Scotland. There she dumped the young woman in a field and drove home.

Eventually Molly was arrested, sent for trial, found guilty and sentenced. Her lawyers were chaotic with many unexplained changes happening at the last minute. She said the trial passed in a blur for her, with little understanding of what was happening. By this time she was pregnant, the pregnancy a result of an encounter with a local boy. Naively Molly thought that being pregnant would soften the judge's heart. This never works. Instead she was given a three and a half year sentence which meant that she would serve 18 months in prison. Now there was not only the pregnancy to worry about (to keep or abort the baby, as the boyfriend wished), the prison sentence, but also the threat of being deported back to the Caribbean because of the violence of her crime.

Children who are not born in Britain, but come to join their parents are in a very vulnerable position with regard to their citizenship. By the time Molly, not a British citizen, was convicted she was in danger of being deported because of the length of her sentence. This indicates how hard it is for the parents to keep their children in mind enough to ensure their right to remain in Britain by taking the necessary legal steps to protect them.

Thanks to the excellent health care and midwifery service in prison Molly's pregnancy proceeded smoothly. As often happens, she adapted well to the prison routine using the therapy on offer and making friends with the other women. Like most of the women she responded to the prison structure of definite meal times, scheduled activities and the absence of abusive boyfriends and parents. She looked healthy and was taking care of herself. Her hair grew and her skin radiated wellbeing.

Her son was born with much family excitement and support. The family visited her in the hospital bringing baby supplies and lavish presents. Even her boyfriend seemed involved and happy to have a son. Of course this is the easy bit. Once the excitement gave way to routine, the family interest and support evaporated. Molly was back in prison questioning why she even had a son and why his father took no interest in either of them. Although her dedication to breastfeeding continued she began to look frail and very vulnerable. Visits from her family, greatly looked forward to, often failed, bringing back memories of waiting in vain for her father. The boyfriend's promise of financial support did not materialise, neither did the supplies he promised to send in for them both.

Grimly Molly would talk about the future and wonder how she would support herself and her son. Listening to a breastfeeding young mother describe the way she would have to go back to working as a lap dancer was profoundly disturbing. The exploitation of women's bodies for financial gain stirred up discussions of slavery in the group. Molly felt far from free. In addition to these financial concerns was the very real possibility that Molly and her son would be deported back to an island where they no longer had ties or family relations.

In an attempt to interest her boyfriend in their son Molly would send him to stay with the boyfriend who would at times forget to come and collect him from the prison. When the father did remember to collect his son he would turn his phone off for the entire weekend so no contact could be made by Molly to see if her son was ok. This was torture for her. It is not hard to imagine the impact of such poor planning on a young baby who has been taken away from his mother and his familiar surroundings for a weekend. Molly was hoping the baby would stimulate some interest in his father. She was disappointed. The young man had no interest in his son and shrank away from contact. It was too much for him.

Despite all that Molly knew from her own experience of disinterested fathers her hope blinded her to the discouraging reality that her own son's father would be unreliable and not interested in him. While in the therapy group we explored her own sense of abandonment and struggles as a mother the legal side of her situation grew. Luckily the charity Hibiscus was able to find her a very good immigration lawyer, but Molly's immigration status was not clear. Having a boyfriend who was so clearly unwilling to provide family life for Molly and her son weakened her chance of staying in the UK.

Talking together one day, Molly said that the solicitor had asked her if there was any reason she could not go back to the Caribbean island. Molly said that there was no reason; she had not had any problems there. Shocked, I said "What about the fact that you were raped when you were a child and you feared for your safety there?" Molly looked at me open mouthed with disbelief. "I never told anyone but you about that.... It is shameful. I am not telling about that now." I think this shows how much abused children blame and disenfranchise themselves; instead of outrage Molly felt only shame and humiliation as if it were easier to blame herself than to rage at a mother who had left her unprotected and vulnerable. Unprotected and vulnerable was the state she was in now with her own child. Despite the solicitor assuring Molly that any information about past difficulties on the island would make her claim to remain in the UK stronger, Molly was not budging.

Time for release approached bringing with it massive uncertainty. Where would she live? How would she support herself and her son? Could she get a job with a criminal record for violence? As often happens as release nears, Molly began to unravel. She made increasingly desperate attempts to involve her son's father and greater pleas to the extended family for support. All fell on deaf ears.

However, with the prison staff's encouragement, Molly prepared to leave. We talked about her fears and what she thought she had learned. She was able to say how much not having a father had hurt her and how much she had missed having a family that could protect her. She could understand what led to her offence and how her mind could just "go blank" when she felt humiliated and ashamed. She was able to grieve for the lost childhood while hoping not to repeat this for her son who she could see needed and loved her. Like many of the young mothers she left prison with promises to keep in touch and a large, slightly defensive smile on her face.

Weeks later she rang me during the mother and baby group and left a message. Clearly she had kept the time and the day in her mind. When we spoke she told me that she was getting on very well and that she had been granted leave to remain in the UK. She also asked if she could come and see me again at the prison. Delighted we made a date.

Coming into the visitors' centre Molly was gleaming, as was her son, resplendent in new clothes and a magnificent buggy. Proud of her new wig and her new possessions, Molly was distant and distracted as if she had disappeared under piles of wrapping paper. She told me that all was going so well, but it was like listening to a voice from across the water. She said that she would like to start having therapy again at the prison and could she do 'Through the Gate' work? I said we could definitely think about this and we arranged a time to meet and discuss it the following week.

Any guesses? No, she did not attend the following week. All the phone numbers that she had given me were also dead. What happened? Was it too far to travel – or was there an even more daunting and difficult journey that she could not face? While I have learned to keep my hopes under control I was very sad not to see her again and can only wonder where she and her son are today.

So, what, if anything does this very brief story tell us? One of my thoughts has to do with the trans-generational impact of slavery with its fractured families and broken chains of relating. Molly lost both of her parents and then her island home all in the hope of reunion. But reunion with what when there had not been a union in the first place? Forced by economic necessity and the unbearable weight of their own early experience Molly's parents were not able to provide a home in their own minds for their children. Bereft of adult protection, Molly, like many of the young girls around her, was plunged into a world of sexual violence and bullying – taking turns being either the victim or perpetrator. To this she replied in kind, identifying with the aggressor. No one would hurt her own sister. Molly tried to protect her sister, but ended up badly hurting another young woman, her own child and herself. Into this chaos her son had been born, again to a fraught mother and a father for whom he was of no interest.

28

Prison provided respite for Molly – paradoxically perhaps a place where she could learn to think about herself in relationship with others. Physically safe she had time to try and put her experience into a story that she could understand. Becoming curious about herself and her origins, Molly's narrative developed insight and depth as she began to think about her own mind and to question where her thoughts came from and what the consequences of her actions would be. Prison narratives are not fairy tales. Nor is the therapist the fairy godmother. Working with such vulnerable, damaged and damaging women seldom has a happy-ever-after ending. But along the way I believe that a sense of reality emerges along with a capacity to think, meaning giving some hope that the future does not have to be a repeat of the past.

Prison uses separation as punishment. The impact of imprisonment can be seen in some statistics that I hope will illuminate the current state of female offending. Also I include these with the hope that they will add context to Molly's individual story.

Statistics tell stories, too. Action for Prisoners' Families (www.prisonersfamilies.org.uk) and Women in Prison (www.womeninprison.org.uk) are the source of valuable statistics.

Britain has the highest prison population in Europe. The total prison population is at an all-time high of 80.000. Men commit the majority of crimes. There are approximately 5,000 women in prison at present. This affects over 17,000 children who are separated from their mothers in the UK.

Many children go into care as a result of the mother's imprisonment. The majority of these children lose their homes and change schools several times. A child with a mother in prison is 13 times more likely to go into a care than a child living with a parent. Having a mother in prison increases the chance of the child going to prison. At present the approximate cost of a year in prison is £45,000. How can we break this cycle or deprivation?

Foreign national women account for approximately 20 per cent of the female prison population. It is hard to tell how many children of foreign nationals are separated from their mothers. Many foreign national women have told me that their children have no idea what country their mothers are in. Other foreign nationals tell their family they are "working abroad", and do not return for years given the long length of their sentence. One mother from Jamaica gave her baby born in prison up for adoption. Given the long length of her sentence she could not face taking the child away from England when her 13 year sentence ended.

For drugs mules the lives of their children are endangered by the drug dealers. Threats from the dealers make it impossible for the women to stop carrying drugs for fear of what will happen at home. One Nigerian mother told me that when she had tried to stop carrying drugs their farmhouse was burnt to the ground. Sadly slavery is not a thing of the past.

Society punishes through separation. Therapy is an attempt to reunite fragmented parts of the self. Who knows if the therapy helped Molly? Will she be able to mother her son in a more thoughtful, protecting way than her own mother was able to do? By "giving sorrow words" in her therapy, will she be able to provide something new, rather than repeat the pattern of abandonment, suffering and neglect? Will her life be better because of the therapy? I will never know for sure. But I do know she and I both tried.

References

Arnold, E. (2012) *Working with Families of African Caribbean Origin, Understanding Issues around Immigration and Attachment.* London, Jessica Kingsley Publishers.
Ryde, J. (2009) *Being White in the Helping Professions.* London, Jessica Kingsley Publications.
Williams, A.H. (1998) *Cruelty, Violence and Murder, Understanding the Criminal Mind.* London, Karnac Books.
www.prisonersfamilies.org.uk
www.womeninprison.org.uk

4. How nurture protects children

Applying the principles of nurture to life in custodial institutions

Jim Rose

Introduction

The title of this chapter, *How nurture protects children* is a pointer towards the importance of attachment theory and the principles of nurture not just as a set of ideas for informing practice, but as a basis for influencing policy making for children, young people and families; in education, social care, health, including mental health and youth justice. [11]

In recent years, there has been a dramatic growth in our understanding of attachment theory and in the amount of supporting research data available in the areas of neuro-science and brain development.

We are well aware that attachment behaviours are common to all mammals and that these behaviours typify the early experiences of mothers and babies in the animal world. Without the protection of their mother and other adults, baby mammals cannot survive; either they fall victim to a predator or they starve. The length of time that this dependency lasts is variable, but it is always a crucial period determining rates of survival into adulthood. For human

---

[11] Rose 2010

infants similar rules apply, but there are qualitative differences to be found in the relationship between a human infant and its mother. It is these differences, in the nature and quality of the inter-actions between mother and baby, that significantly influence the processes of later development. The linking of the biological force of attachment with the physiological and chemical reactions of the emerging infant brain creates the conditions for each child's unique emotional, psychological and social development.

In essence, a child learns through the primary attachment relationship the answers to certain key questions: Is the world a safe place for me? Can I rely on this person and other adults to look after me? Will my needs be met when I need them to be? Will there always be someone there for me when I need protection? The answers that a child receives to these questions contribute to the formation of what John Bowlby referred to as an 'internal working model', i.e. a view based on experience about how safe the world is and what their place in it is likely to be.

In their first year of life babies learn how their needs are met and their anxieties contained through the protective, nurturing and soothing responses of their mothers, who either provide an immediate response to their expressed needs, or attend to them within a sufficiently short enough time. These experiences are the basis for the formation of a *secure attachment* between a mother and her baby, a relationship which is crucial for later development and which will significantly influence the child's capacity for learning.

The core ideas from attachment theory, along with an ever increasing and available body of knowledge about the neuro-science of brain development, are critical in considering the impact of imprisonment on parent – child relationships. If the conditions are not met for the development of a 'good enough' secure attachment and the child learns maladaptive ways of coping with the absence of, or rejection by, a primary care giver then there are inevitably serious consequences for that child, which may later manifest in anti-social behaviours; in difficulties in forming and sustaining relationships; in low educational achievement and with an increased potential for violence and deviancy. Research amongst adult male prisoners shows a high prevalence of early attachment difficulties, while we know that many of the children (aged 10to 17) locked up in secure establishments have been previously separated from their families with periods of time spent 'in care', multiple placements and frequent changes of carer.

Who does custody affect?

Ideas from attachment and nurture have particular resonance when thinking about the circumstances of women in custodial institutions. However, they also provide the framework for shaping the regimes which are delivered on a day-today basis in every custodial setting. These include adult males, young men and women (18 to 21 years) and some 2,500 or so children, both boys and girls, under the age of 18 years. The relevance of attachment theory and the principles of nurture are perhaps most keenly realised when consideration is given to the impact that a custodial sentence has on the critical relationship between parents and their children and the damaging effects of enforced separations on the quality of these relationships, in both the short and longer term.

The plight of those women who are sentenced to terms of imprisonment continues to stir up heated debate. Many reformers demand the total abolition of custody for women, whilst others call for alternative, dedicated small units to be developed for those instances when detention is required for public protection. All agree, however, that for the vast majority of women, community sentences should be the preferred option for courts. As recently as March 2012 the Chief Inspector of Prisons, Nick Hardwick, said in a lecture: "Prisons, particularly as they are currently run, are simply the wrong place for so many of the distressed, damaged or disturbed women they hold... I think the treatment and conditions in which a small minority of the most disturbed women are held is... simply unacceptable. I think – I hope – we will look back on how we treated these women in years to come, aghast and ashamed."

The lecture was delivered to mark the fifth anniversary of a report by Baroness Corston.[12] At the lecture she

---

[12] *A report by Baroness Jean Corston of a review of women with particular vulnerabilities in the criminal justice system,* 2007.

acknowledged that some progress had been made, although she went on to say: "The courts are still sending too many women to prison. The levels of self-harming are utterly horrifying. It's the one thing where these women feel they have some form of control. Everything else is beyond their control or impossible to deal with."

Although the overall prison population has continued to grow, the number of women sentenced to custody has dropped slightly. Nevertheless, at any one time there are around 4,500 adult women locked up in prison – approximately 8,000 each year. This represents about five per cent of the total prison population, a small percentage but a significant number. Nevertheless, the consequences of the relatively low numbers of women in prison are the familiar problems for a 'minority' group in a large population, i.e. the allocation of sufficient resources and the availability of local provision. Sentences for women are generally short-term (under eight months on average) and are mainly for non-violent offences. The argument for a reduced use of custody for women is additionally strengthened by the fact that, for what are relatively minor offences, women are more likely to receive a custodial sentence than their male counter-parts.

Outcomes for short custodial sentences, in terms of effect on family relationships and for work undertaken by community based services are generally poor and certainly disproportionate to any benefit that may result from a term in prison. There is, however, one further and undeniably shocking fact: while women may form a statistically small part of the overall prison population, 50 per cent of all the episodes of self-harm recorded by the prison service involve women. This statistic reinforces the inappropriatèness of prison for the majority of convicted women, highlighting the enormous distress experienced by women in custody and the failure of custodial regimes to address their very considerable needs.

Sixty per cent of women in custody have children from whom they are separated during the period of their sentence and around three per cent of women have their babies with them in prison. For those mothers who leave children in the community the pain of the separation, whatever the ages of their children, can have devastating effects. The disruption to family life often exacerbates already troubled relationships and increases the risk factors for the children's later involvement in delinquent behaviour. We have already identified the problem of providing local units for the relatively small number of women sentenced to custody and as a direct consequence of the distance they are placed away from home, visiting is often difficult for families to maintain on a regular basis.

On a positive note, there are some prisons that have developed imaginative facilities to encourage family visits which mean that visits can have real benefits, e.g. by arranging informal family days with activities, allowing mothers to spend longer period of time in direct contact with their children. However, in many establishments visiting arrangements are too often dominated by overly intrusive security procedures, e.g. searching and the presence of closed circuit television (CCTV), rather than providing opportunities for the time to enable a meaningful reunion for the parent and child.

The presence of babies with their mothers in the prison setting, albeit in specialist units, inevitably raises questions about the nature of the regimes provided. Given what we know about the critical significance of attachment in the first hours, days and months of mother- baby relationships and the importance of ensuring a stable and nurturing environment for the continuing healthy growth of the infant, it is clearly essential that these mothers and babies are offered the best opportunities in which to foster close and loving relationships. One of the aims of early intervention is to break inter-generational cycles of delinquent or anti-social behaviour but, however well designed the units may be, it is hard to see how a restrictive prison environment realistically offers mothers and babies the right sort of start to a stable family life.

But, as we have already indicated, it is not just mothers and babies who are affected by the custodial experience. The issues of separation and disruption to family life affect all groups in custodial institutions. The majority of men in prison (including a high number of young male offenders) are fathers, with responsibilities for children who remain outside the prison walls whilst the custodial sentence is being served. In addition, there are also significant numbers of children locked up in secure establishments.

Over time there has been increasing awareness, supported by research findings, about the importance of fathers in family life. This is often framed in a negative perspective, i.e. about the impact that the lack of a strong male role model has on children, especially boys, without emphasising the growing evidence that the consistent presence of a male figure makes a specific and positive contribution to a child's overall development. A male who plays an active part in the life of a child complements the qualities brought to the parenting role by the female, thereby providing a more holistic, nurturing experience.

In the report, *Dying to Belong* [13] it is stated that: "The absence of a positive male role model in the home has frequently been noted as a driver for male gang membership. As one London YOT worker put it, 'there's a big issue with fathers being at home and the relationship that a father needs to have with his son'." [14]

Using as an example the work of Melvyn Davies who runs a charity which provides support and practical guidance for boys making the transition into adulthood, the report notes two key consequences for boys growing up with either physically or emotionally absent fathers: the rejection and inadequacy they feel as a result of growing up in a fatherless household, which is often internalised, creating huge resentment and anger and the absence of positive masculinity being modelled to them, forcing them to 'learn' their masculinity from traditional 'alpha' male imagery, readily available through popular media.

---

[13] The Centre for Social Justice, 2009
[14] CSJ 2009, p. 98

Quoting directly from Melvyn Davies the report continues: "Much of their behaviour (boy gang members) was linked to their need to prove themselves as young men. Which in some ways is common to a lot of boys' development but in their case it was far more punctuated by the fact that there wasn't a father figure. So they needed to prove themselves and that made them a lot more vulnerable. So there was a lot more risk-taking behaviour, there was a lot of standing up to people and not being able to back down and feeling 'This is what I'm supposed to do'. They had a very narrow definition of what it means to be a man and masculinity, because again, they had not been growing up with men in their lives in a personal way and so they were absorbing the images from the media that they were seeing... If you look at the underlying reasons for a lot of the violence, a lot of the crime...it stems back to his understanding of himself as a man. 'It's what I'm supposed to do. I can't let it buoy me up. I've got to represent being a man'." [15]

While there are many more reasons for absent fathers than imprisonment, the evidence is clear that the vulnerability of a young person to join in delinquent behaviour or to seek gang membership is increased by having a parent, most usually the father, in prison. As Melvyn Davies points out, the current societal conflicts

---

[15] CSJ 2009. P. 98

about maleness or what it means 'to be a man' are particularly relevant for thinking about the effect of imprisonment on boys and young males.

Children in custody

The profile of young people in secure settings, including Young Offender Institutions makes for salutary reading: "Secure units are dealing with young people who are likely to have had disrupted and disturbed experiences of family life from a very early age and many have been subject to various and often multiple forms of abuse by adults from whom they might have expected better. For a large number of these young people this has resulted in episodes of being in care, running away and fractured links with any form of stable home life. A significant number of the young people have had difficulties at school with both teachers and other children. This has resulted later on in either exclusion or truancy with the associated problems of having large amounts of unstructured time on their hands and contact with, or being influenced by anti-social peer groups. A high number have experimented with various forms of drugs or alcohol which in some cases means becoming dependent upon these substances.

Many young people have long standing mental health problems and there are a significant number who have Attention Deficit Disorder. A high percentage have attempted self-harm and /or had suicidal thoughts and many have attempted to act on these. Young people in secure units may present with one, some or all of these problems in any combination, with varying degrees of severity and differences in age of onset." [16]

Young people placed in secure accommodation, having been sentenced to custody, often have to be placed some distance from their local communities and separated from whatever family links they have managed to retain. Over 50 per cent of these young people have experienced periods of time in care in foster placements or children's homes with all too frequent changes in carer. In these circumstances it is essential that the daily regime within which they live while in custody is shaped on principles and practices that best provide for addressing their complex and multiple needs and provide opportunities for learning and for the development of positive, pro-social relationships.

What should custody provide?

Much of our current criminal justice policy is based on ideas about punishment and retribution with a predominant emphasis on public protection and risk management. It is certainly the case that the effects of crime on victims and the damage caused by anti-social behaviour should never be minimised. However, serious thinking about rehabilitation or achieving real change in the behaviour of offenders needs to be informed by our knowledge about the importance of early attachment relationships and the on-going processes

---

[16] Rose 2002. P. 33

of child development. Relationship based practices, drawing upon the ideas of attachment theory, provide the most fruitful possibilities for engaging with offender groups, especially young people. Furthermore, the principles of nurture, which have emerged over the years as the cornerstone of nurture group practice, provide a sound basis for regime development within young offender custodial institutions.

Nurture groups were originally developed as an intervention with children in primary schools, but increasingly their value is being acknowledged in secondary schools as well as in other settings with young people, (Rose 2010). There is a growing body of research evidence showing nurture groups to be a very effective way of engaging with disaffected children and young people and how their success derives from being grounded in relational practice that embraces a clear set of principles and values, i.e. the establishing of a matrix of relationships between adults and children in a secure and safe environment; understanding children's needs developmentally rather than as symptoms of pathology; regarding children's behaviour as a communication about the condition of their internal world; encouraging the use of language for the expression of emotion, reducing the need for acting out; improving children's self-esteem through structured routines and activities that offer opportunities for achievement and lastly a recognition of the importance and meaning of transitions in the lives of children and young people.

Custodial institutions for young people

If these principles were to be rigorously applied to regime design in custodial institutions for young people they would enable staff to be more confident in addressing the underlying issues around attachment which directly influence so much of these young people's behaviour. In this section of the chapter we argue that custodial regimes need to be built on relational models of practice that encourage high levels of adult – child contact within a stable, predictable routine of daily activities. The creation of a safe physical environment is the foundation for the development of a psychologically safe and containing environment that is necessary for any therapeutic work to be effective.

While improvements to the daily regime in Young Offender Institutions are essential there are a number of other factors that are also vital to address if a custodial experience is to have positive impact in a young person's life. Perhaps the most important one of these is achieving continuity in the relationship between work undertaken in the custodial setting with the services provided for the young person in the community, both before and after the period of imprisonment. By its very nature a custodial sentence removes a young person from their community and away from their family. Of course, it may be that these relationships are both the source and cause of their delinquent behaviour, but the fact remains that post-custody the majority of young people are most likely to return to the situation in which they were previously living.

In my experience as the Professional Adviser to HM Prison Service, advising on the placement and management of young people sentenced to long term custody for very serious crimes, it became clear that whilst there were a few young people who committed a 'one-off' serious offence and received a long prison sentence, the vast majority of this group of young people had been known to a wide range of services and agencies over many years. Furthermore, whilst it was true that each young person had their own unique story to tell and that their particular history shaped their specific behaviour, a common factor across many of these accounts was the lack of a consistent adult figure through their childhood.

This combination of factors, i.e. being well known to social care and youth justice agencies, along with the absence of a consistent, single adult figure, emphasises the importance of maintaining continuity and stability in young people lives, not just in terms of services and programmes, but in the key adult figures who work with them or look after them, e.g. foster carers.

Overcoming structural difficulties in areas such as terms of employment and differentiating between professional roles and boundaries in order to provide continuity of relationships is a pre-requisite for ensuring a smooth transition for young people going into and coming out of secure establishments. It is still regrettably the case that, despite many improvements to the youth justice system, a young person can reach the release point in their sentence with little or no idea about where they are going to be living or who is going to meet them when the 'gates' open. Given that we know that what happens in the first 24 hours after release can determine the success or otherwise of the post-release programme, it is clearly critical that there is co-ordinated and comprehensive planning between custodial and community based staff regarding a young person's on-going programme.

Regime change

Arguably, the current daily regime in Young Offender Institutions exacerbates rather than ameliorates the problems of the vulnerable adolescents placed within. These units, which house the vast majority of young people in custody, are generally characterised by large numbers of young people, low staff ratios that offer few opportunities for positive individual contact between adults and young people, limited educational activity and with a culture of control that is marked by a high use of physical restraint.

All of these features militate against the creation of a safe and secure environment in which young people can feel sufficiently emotionally and physically contained in order to begin to confront their problems. The physical separation from family and community that is the result of a custodial sentence is likely to be experienced more deeply by a young person with attachment issues in a setting that heightens feelings of isolation and evokes anxious feelings about personal safety.

In my role as Professional Adviser I engaged in numerous discussions with both staff and young people in secure establishments and the above concerns, i.e. a fear of isolation and of personal attack, were consistently highlighted by both groups. For staff, the feelings were expressed in terms of their being abandoned by colleagues and physically assaulted by the 'inmates'. For young people, the anxiety was located in the experience of being locked away alone in a cell for long periods of time, especially at night, and also a fear of being bullied by other young people and staff.

In order to address these issues, especially those affecting young people, it is essential for staff to develop sensitivity and awareness about the nature of their work in the secure environment, in particular about the underlying needs of the young people in their care.

The nurture principle, 'all behaviour is communication', provides a key for staff in looking beyond the presenting 'bad' behaviour of a young person and towards an understanding that there may be some deeper communication about that young person's experience and history. This kind of insight is extremely helpful for staff struggling to make sense of a young person's behaviour or trying to find a way to manage it safely.

It is also helpful for staff in the generality of their routine work in the secure setting: Staff lock and open doors dozens of times each day, yet are quite likely never to think about what impact these actions might have on a young person who is anxious about being left alone in their cell. What does it mean for a child who has been abused or abandoned to be shut away with a banged door and a clunky turn of a key? What message is conveyed by the cheery 'goodnights' or 'see you in pub' called out by a member of staff to colleagues going off duty? The provision of a safe and containing environment does not just happen but requires committed managers who are able to ensure that their staff have time to think about the details of their practice, not just when they are involved in so-called 'therapeutic work,' but in the day-to-day delivery of the ordinary routines that are the bed-rock of residential life.

Applying the principles of nurture to life in a secure custodial institution yields a rich harvest in terms of practice: we have referred to understanding behaviour as a communication and the important transition that occurs when a young person leaves the secure establishment and returns to the community. Of similar importance is the transition from community to custody, when young people are especially vulnerable on the first night that they spend alone in a locked room or cell. The potential risk of self-harming is increased not only for young people who may have a history of such behaviour, but for a good number of others as well who find the sense of isolation frightening or overwhelming.

All establishments pay particular attention to this aspect of their regime, whilst some have developed special 'first night' procedures identifying certain items that young people may wish to have in their cells to help keep them calm and reassured about their safety, e.g. reading materials, a radio, and paper and pens for writing or drawing.

Another nurture principle is the 'classroom as a safe base'; this principle links the physical design and furnishing of the group room with the psychological safe-base provided by the adult staff. The reference is back towards attachment theory with the location of an infant's safe base in their relationship with the primary carer. The challenge for custodial establishments is how they can help staff to make the connections between maintaining the physical security of the buildings and developing positive relationships with the young people a conscious part of their daily work. This requires a different way of thinking about the custodial experience and the nature of the work that staff are required to undertake in their daily duties.

Conclusion

This chapter has focused mainly on young people and how their needs may best be met in a custodial setting. However, the ideas of attachment and the principles nurture apply to all settings and therefore to all people who are sentenced to custody and sent to prison establishments.

We need policies and management systems that allow and encourage practitioners working in the secure estate to be able to think about the notions of security and containment in terms of their psychological meaning rather than just in regard to locking up and shutting away. Prison regimes need to be refocused in order to address the profound and pervasive attachment difficulties that affect the majority of adults and young people in secure establishments and to provide the necessary experiences and relationships that offer the most effective kind of support and help to prevent reoffending.

While custody continues to exist as a sentencing option for courts it is necessary to argue and lobby about the nature of the custodial experience, to describe alternative models for the design of the daily regimes in secure establishments and to propose different ways in which those regimes may best be delivered. However, in the final analysis, the most effective opportunities for strengthening parent - child relationships will only realistically be achieved by a dramatic reduction in the uses of custody, particularly for women and young people. To achieve this it is essential to create a broader range of credible community programmes as viable alternatives to a custodial sentence.

Above all, what is required is a different way of thinking at policy level about the needs of children, young people and adults in order to promote healthy emotional development, encourage learning and develop positive rather than anti-social behaviour. Research evidence about the far-reaching significance of attachment and nurture in the healthy growth and development of children and young people belies once and for all the criticism that these are just 'soft and woolly' concepts that have no place in criminal justice policy. They are, in fact, critical components of the theoretical and practice frameworks that are essential if the real issues that we are all concerned about for parents and children in custody are to be fully and effectively addressed.

References

Baroness Jean Corston, (2007) *A report of a review of women with particular vulnerabilities in the criminal justice system,* London, Home Office

Bennathan, M. and Rose, J. (2008) *All About Nurture Groups,* London, The Nurture Group Network

Colley, D. (2009) Nurture groups in secondary schools, *Emotional and Behavioural Difficulties,* 14:4, 291 - 300

Cooper, P., Whitebread, D. (2007) 'The Effectiveness of Nurture Groups on Student Progress: Evidence from a National Research Study', *Emotional and Behavioural Difficulties,* 12:3, 171–190.

Rose, J. (2002) *Working with Young People in Secure Accommodation - From Chaos to Culture,* London, Brunner – Routledge

Rose, J. (2010) *How Nurture Protects Children* London, Responsive Solutions UK Ltd.

The Centre for Social Justice (2009) *Dying to Belong*

5. Breaking the Chain
The applicability and quality of the Growth Journey

Richard Uglow

This chapter is about a programme that we call the 'Growth Journey'. It is a 10 week development program, which has been delivered in a male prison environment in the United Kingdom for the last three years. The intention of the Growth Journey is to start prisoners along the path to crime-free rehabilitation and sustainable living thereafter.

At the start of this chapter there is an introduction to the Growth Journey, its context, how it has been used, and some of the benefits. Then the body of the chapter, shares with you the efficacy, or the quality of intervention, that we at Enrichyou use to address the whole person, and we share some case studies to bring that to life. Lastly, I summarise the principles of why the Growth Journey works, so that it gives you some encouragement, and hopefully some inspiration to look again at how you use what you do in developing people; and perhaps in the most difficult contexts.

I am a master practitioner in NLP – that is Neuro-linguistic Programming – which, in simple terms in the context of 'The Growth Journey', is a coaching, therapeutic, counselling-type discipline. I am also a fully qualified NLP coach who has been in practice for seven years and this enables me and anyone qualified to this level to work with the whole person.

This chapter has been created from a transcript of the actual presentation I delivered to the conference and so much of it is in the first person.

* * * * *

The Growth Journey

I had no intention whatsoever of working in a prison environment, when in 2007 a prison chaplain came up to me one day, with a little glint in his eye, and said, "Why don't you come to the prison in Lincolnshire that I work at, I need some help". Being a helpful sort of chap, I said, "I'm happy to come along and talk"; and so, I turned up at the Lincolnshire prison on a cold, bleak afternoon, and just sat down and spoke to the chaplain about his issues and concerns. He described himself as a lowly prison chaplain, who had no money and no resources to work with; and so he was really reaching out to the local community for help to work with the men in his care.

And so I said to the prison chaplain, "Why don't we have a conversation with some of the guys? Why don't we talk to some of the men and find out what it is that they want; find out what some of their thoughts and feelings are." So we agreed that I would come back and talk to a group of prisoners, and that happened on about three occasions, across about three months.

At that time we were really trying to find out how best to help, particularly the prisoners. After the third visit, while safely out of public view, I collapsed into unconscious, uncontrollable tears. The travesty of human brokenness and the ignorance of our prison system, affected me deeply. I could see a production line of wasted lives and this was the end of the line and nothing was happening to address the root cause of the men's issues. I was 46 years old and I had no idea that prison was like 'landfill for human beings'. It was only through tears that the scale of this madness could be expressed through me. It would bring most of you with a heart to tears also to really listen to and understand some of the stories that these men share. Don't misunderstand me: there is definitely a line that needs to be drawn that says: "no", criminal behaviour is not acceptable in a grown-up society; but a conviction should be the start of a process of learning, understanding, development and human growth if the men are ready to choose a different level of life.

The rights and wrongs of the prison or justice system, anywhere in the world, but particularly in the UK, are not the primary concern of this chapter. We have in our prisons a well-intentioned service, but which plays out, for many prisoners, as little more than bed and breakfast. Later on there is one person I am going to describe to you, who had been rotting in jail for 18 years, and in 10 weeks came back from being an empty shell with a human body, to being somebody who was absolutely human and full of life. Why do we let this happen?

A 'Growth Journey' is what I know how to do. Consequently I know that at least 80 per cent of the prisoner population would be able to find crime-free living with the right help and processes. The Growth Journey that I started in the October 2007 has this at its core. On a Growth Journey we engage with the individual person, who are still men, even though they may have the label 'prisoner', they are men who originally started life, like all of us having been created in the image and likeness of the God that we cannot see. Their human lives were not formed fully, properly or became corrupted along the way. I listen at a deep level and to all levels of their experience, and at the right time, ask each person to describe the intention of what it is that they would like their Growth Journey to be about. I ask them who they want to become at the end of it, I ask them to create their better level of life and future.

Let me give you an example of what that could be; a 39 year old man, who was in prison for aggravated burglary, violence, and manslaughter, wanted – when we listened to him – to move on from being a boy to become a man. He had not grown up, he had never had the opportunity to grow into manhood, but at 39, it was not too late. It is never too late. Another one of the men on the Growth Journey wanted to find "the real me". He was 52 years old, and he had felt that he actually did not know who he was. He had never known who he was. He had never really found out what it was to be a human being. These are just some of the deeper examples about what people can ask for.

What we can be absolutely certain of is that the men never ask for 'a negative presentation'. They never say, I would like to stop committing fraud or I would like to stop being violent. The criminal behaviour is always the symptom of something deeper. All Growth Journey attendees find the deeper cause and learn to express the road ahead 'positively' by finding 'new resources' inside them, rather than stopping something that has external behaviours describe by society as a crime.

The latter would be as successful as people deciding to stop smoking or to lose weight in the New Year. Often these initiatives don't succeed because it does not address the deeper levels of why smoking or weight was gained in the first place. Criminal behaviours stop or start to cease, but by finding the right level of missing pieces to focus on.

I use the language advisedly because we should not shy away from it. What I ask each person on a Growth Journey to do, is to find the soul root cause of the nature of their issues, and the systemic nature of the issue, that is how it affects any or all human beings that they come into contact with. If we can help someone to work with who they are at that level, then the whole of the human being comes to life. If we deal with the symptoms at a superficial level, then what happens is; we all limp on together.

When we listen to what we call 'the intention', and we elicit that intention from each person, we help them get to express what we call the soul-root cause of the crime. We then commit to that person that we will journey with them until their intention is manifest, i.e. it has become a reality −

that is, they have reached a point where they say that now I am in the examples above, "I am now a man, not a boy" or "I have found the real me".

This has been used and proven over 10 years, not only in a prison capacity, but also with kids with learning difficulties in schools, in a well-being context, and we have used it with senior business people, and in family settings too.

So, this is the Growth Journey.

The efficacy and quality of the intervention

Let us now look at the essence of why this intervention works, and what we really need to be thinking about for any of us to follow this path and to replicate what we have been doing, particularly in the prison environment, but also over these 10 years in all of life's situations.

What I am about to describe is not academic; it is not something that, if you are an academic, is the fullest intellectual wrapping of this subject. For me, the initial guidance contained in academic books exists, and we are taught a level of knowledge and a certain level of engagement, but this chapter is really about sharing the essence of the actual experience gained from sitting in front of, and working with men who have committed crimes, in a real-life situation, where the theory ends, and the practise and real-life starts.

When we are doing a Growth Journey in prisons, we are thinking about the people and ourselves in four levels:

At level one we call this the criminal behaviour: it is the behaviour, the things that we see people doing, which are dysfunctional, and it is damaging normally – that is why in society it is called crime. So for example, criminal behaviour is someone committing fraud, or it is somebody joy riding, or it is somebody doing something which may endanger other people's lives. At a society level, this **is** something we should say no to; but that is the tip of the ice-berg, that is the symptom.

At level two in the working Growth Journey, we call it the human group behaviour. For all of us are either 'not whole' in some way and at some level or we are broken or we are not working to the fullest capacity and capability of the soul, – we are all learning to find out what it is to be a full human being. In our normal society group situations, either in a family, or in a social group, what happens is that we are a mirror to each other, and we give each other feedback and we set healthy boundaries where we can contain and tolerate each other's learning, brokenness, foibles and transgressions too. This mostly happens within the norms of happiness and some level of positive self-esteem. Usually a bit of conflict happens along the way too. However, in some situations, the people or the group are not strong enough or functional enough to support the level of dysfunctional behaviour. It is at this point that we need to go to a deeper level of engagement with the person, and often this requires some level of wisdom like family aunts and uncles or even professional help.

So then we may need to go to the next level of intervention, level three which is the human inner behaviour. And again, in a prison setting, when we are working with a prisoner and we move into what we call level three, we are talking about leading the person to a place where they access the command of their own inner 'good and natural' capacity, where they have got a self-awareness about their own talents, they have an understanding about how **to be** in certain contexts and environments; so for example for men in a male environment, swearing is typically ok, and there is often lots of male banter – which is acceptable – but when you go to visit granny, or in front of mum, then we learn to change our behaviour to suit the situation.

We need to learn to be able to be flexible with the levels of life, and this is about being in command of our inner behaviours, and this for me is the life journey of self-management, and it is a process which is constantly in flux, because life throws up different situations and challenges, and we need to respond. Often, our prisoner group is very under-resourced in their capacity to engage with their greater depths inside and with the ability to be flexible in different situations.

Then, we will need to operate at the fourth level of intervention this is what I call the spiritual, or soul level of intervention; this is where we have or have not engaged in active and life giving faith. Whether you believe in something that people might call God, or spirit or not, at this point, all I am going to assert to you is that it will limit you if you do not have an understanding of 'it' – that is God and Spirit – and you will be limiting yourself and not experiencing the fullness of life if you are not 'active in relationship through faith' with the God that we cannot see. My assertion for you is that we are all spiritual beings at the core. There is so much evidence and places to find out the truth of what exists, that to not understand the spiritual world is not to have been shown properly or to not have tried to look hard enough for it. Understandably most of our 'men' are not engaged in life at this level.

The issue for us as human beings is that we probably have not mastered our spirituality in a practical way; people have theories and beliefs, but at a soul level, what is practical is that each person needs to find who they are in purpose, who they are in human design, so that we find our vocation in life and the job that we are born to do. We are not here on planet Earth to have 'employed jobs', to be fodder for a capitalist system, or a communist system, or an inanimate system; we are here as real people, to somehow engage with our essence of what we have inside, and then from that place and self-knowing, 'create', in a peaceful and loving way. What we know as practitioners of the Growth Journey is that when we can assist people to a place where they can find their inner peace, then everything else will start to flourish, and for 'prisoners' their true freedom is found so that they can start to engage in life at the right level and start 'crime-free rehabilitation' by pointing in the right way.

This is the place that we need to do the deep listening from; this is the place where restoration, true restoration and lasting timeless restoration begins. Who of you reading this would not want inner peace, if you could find it and you don't have it all of the time? Who of you reading this would with-hold your own gift of love, service of others and inner peace from those not in your own immediate family circle and not help those who are troubled or struggling in life to find what you have, for themselves?

Let me share just one case study with you

The one I am just going to share with you, that gives you a sense of the efficacy of what is possible here, is to do with a person I am going to call Jim. His name is not Jim, but our work is obviously confidential and his name at this point does not matter; what matters is what happened here. I could get every one of you to a place of tears if I were to describe to you the story that he has described to me. His upbringing in a sense is an utter travesty of the way in which people can still be brought up in life, particularly here in the UK.

By the age of 18 his father, who was unemployed, drunk most days, had a set of rules, which included for example; he was allowed to buy cocaine and deal with drugs, but he was not allowed to leave the needles lying around in the house. He was allowed to steal bicycles as long as he was not caught, and so by the age of 18 you can understand the sort of, the level of humanity that this boy had 'not been' trained to.

But before we judge the parent, the question is, to be in that state, how was the dad trained? Who trained him? How did he get to that lowest level of life guidance? Our point about breaking the chain is this: in the end – there is no point in making the judgement; in the end – all parents bring up the children in the best way they know how to. If that is not the highest level necessary to sustain the fullness of life, then what we need to do is help each other to find the higher gifts of life and not judge their past. Breaking the Chain is about the help and not the judgement. It is the only sure way out of where prisoners find themselves in life. As a society and as successive governments we maintain the 'men' in physical prison and also in spiritual prisons – because of our own society level blindness and judgement.

Let us go back to Jim; by the age of 18, he left home, he was unemployed and was unemployed until the age of 35, where he went in and out of various jobs and casual work, until on a drug and alcohol-fuelled night, he had an argument with a friend and he took out a knife and killed his mate, and was convicted – correctly – of murder at the age of 35.

When I found Jim, he was 52 years old and he had been in all of British jails from High Security Category A, to progressively lesser levels of restriction in Category B, C and D, prisons to a place where he was utterly lifeless. The life had been drained out of him, and he had no hope – he had no sense about a future, or about how to leave the past behind him. For 18 years he sat rotting in our jails at the average annual cost of £40,000 per prisoner. That is £720,000 to £1 million of tax payer's money to look after Jim. After just a 10 week Growth Journey he became a somebody, who was working from the deeper blueprint intended for his life – someone who had found his vocation to work with animals, somebody who was confident enough to start to trust, to engage in a social group – and a somebody - who had put behind him his criminal behaviour. Now, even if the legal punishment in our current society is to serve a jail sentence and for anybody who has murdered, some significant punishment is needed to remedy the crime – there is no need that someone contained physically in a jail, should be prevented from being able to find the spiritual state of inner peace and inner freedom. It is only in this level of restoration that the true healing and remedy takes place. The serving of time for time's sake is an ineffective punishment and at a spiritual level 'unnecessary' if proper restoration happens. It is what happens **in** the time that matters. And so, in the 10 weeks that the Growth Journey happened, Jim transformed himself, with our assistance, at a physical, emotional and spiritual level, into someone who had been healed and freed of his murdering past; the past where his level of childhood upbringing had already destined him for such a future.

And so, going back to the levels of restoration, he had been restored at all four levels – in 10 weeks. So when we look at crime, we need to ask where the crime is really committed; is it at the point of conviction or is in the level of care and guidance that forms the criminal or allows the human being to take the lowest path in life? Did Jim make it to the responsible adult level by the age of 18? No, but our law assumes that this is so.

That level of human transformation is possible. It is what as a society we need to learn how to do. And when we do that, the prison service that costs us all about £11 billion a year, and the people that go through it, will come out with our help and not our judgement, to be contributing members of society, not because we're allowing them to, not even because they're safe, but mostly because they have found for themselves what it is to become a human being. They will have discovered the greater capacities of being whole and will be setting out in a life direction based on their authenticity as written on the soul.

Summary and the principles of the Growth Journey in a nutshell

So on a Growth Journey we connect with each person as a person and don't judge them or label them by their crime; we set intention, we find out what somebody really wants from the authentic deepest part inside them, we help the person to unlock and to restore themselves at any or all of the four levels of life, and the core principle that we work to is: that we elicit the soul root cause of the crime, so that the deepest level of restoration, guided by the person's own highest level of intention – which means that the people will tell us what they really want and need when we are listening to them properly.

As a foundation to whatever they specifically want, we ask each person to aim for a state of inner peace, on a growth journey, and while **they** won't know how to get there, neither will we. In the talking and listening and engagement through committed relationship, we help the person to get to their end game, which will be what they asked for as their intention in the beginning (e.g. like to find the real me).

We manage the presenting issues at the level of the issue, and we work at the pace that the person grows. There is no herding, there is no "my pace because I'm capable and I'm an able human being", it is about what that person is able to do. Yes, there are ups-and-downs, we do not all get it in the first instant. We need patience, some people are very troubled and therefore, we need to work with all the levels of wisdom around physical containment, working with other people and so on, to pace the person as they grow in the way that they had never done before. It is a process of education, training, edification and sanctification.

We are aiming to assist transformation at the deepest level within that person, and in each person. From a prison perspective, 95 per cent of prisoners in the UK are male, with a prison population at any one time of about 80,000. There is a whole system surrounding the prisoner, and beyond each prisoner including wives, families, girlfriends, mothers, fathers, and of course the victims of crime.

The systemic principle is, that if you can address the inner issues at all levels with each person, then fundamentally you can engage in a restorative justice of the systemic level; victims if necessary, the family system, and you can then do it with some level of safety, and some level of greater wisdom, because the person has changed. They are not now the person that committed the crime, and so they can engage in the world in a different way.

When that process sees its fullest conclusion, we end up with the management of – we will call it – reunion; where the person being changed gets back to being normal, – not in a robotic compliant society sense, but normal, in the sense that they have found what it is to become a human being living life from the core and more of the spiritual source of life even if this is at an unconscious level.

The 'separation' inside a person which can happen in most people from the early years because of the environment they were brought up in or found themselves is – can in the extremes - lead to the behaviours of crime. The restoration of that inner brokenness into inner peace and some level of inner wholeness becomes the first process of 're-union'. When inner re-union has occurred the person's external expression and in a prisoner's situation, criminal behaviour will cease and the fullness of life and a positive contribution to society can begin. That is the essence of the Growth Journey and it is the highest efficacy programme we have to be able 'to assist' in breaking the chain that binds those who are not engaged in or experiencing the fullness of life.

If this has been of use to you and you wish to ask more questions about the growth journey or you think it may be of some benefit to you, someone you know or to the prison or working environment which you are leader within, then please e-mail me personally at:

richard.uglow@enrichyou.co.uk or phone me on 08456 126 006 when I or one of my colleagues in the first instance will come back to you to find out the nature of your enquiry just as soon as we are able. You can download other case-studies by visiting the website:

www.enrichyou.co.uk/case-studies.html

An audio of the presentation is also available on the website but has production and postage costs associated with it.

I thank you for reading this chapter.

6. Kinship care and imprisonment
Support for families and friends who step in when parents are imprisoned.

Cherecee Williams

When I was asked to facilitate a workshop on kinship care and imprisonment at this conference, I thought I could fill a number of pages explaining my views, but decided that it might be better to share some of the stories of the people I have worked with. All names mentioned in this chapter have been changed. Before I do this however, I am going to set the scene.

Setting the scene

I work for the charity for prisoners' families, Pact, as the Kinship Care Support Service Manager. The Kinship Care Support Service aims to provide support and advice to family members and friends who care for children whose parents are imprisoned. The ultimate goal of the service is to ensure better outcomes for children by helping to resolve any conflicts between the kinship carers and the imprisoned parents; and to help facilitate contact between children and their imprisoned mothers.

Kinship care is provided when a child has to live away from his or her parental home, and is cared for full-time by a member of the child's extended family or a friend. Kinship care arrangements can arise from many circumstances such as parental substance misuse, mental health issues, migration or imprisonment. When a parent is sent to prison, children are usually cared for by a grandparent, older sibling, aunt, or family friend. Each year it is estimated that 17,700 children are separated from their mothers by imprisonment.[17] When mothers are imprisoned only five per cent of those children remain in their own home. There is a 40 per cent chance that the children will be placed in the care of their grandparents, and a 20 per cent chance that the children will live with other kinship carers.

There are fewer female prison establishments in England and Wales, which means that families visiting a woman in prison often have to travel a lot further. The burden is enormous. Families are, in effect, also serving a sentence. One of the kinship carers I have supported is a disabled grandmother with poor health who is taking care of five grandchildren between the ages of five and 13. Every two weeks she travels a great distance for a one hour visit to see her daughter in prison. She is afraid to seek help, because she believes that if she does, the children will be placed in local authority care.

Another kinship carer is an aunt who is looking after her four nieces and nephews. She is only 27 years old, and wants to start a family of her own, but feels she cannot do so because she has to take care of her sister's children. She travels the six hour round trip from Cardiff to London every

---

[17] Women in Prison, Prison Reform Trust, 2010

other month so that the children can see their mother. She receives some financial support, but not enough to provide the children with everything they need.

What are the major issues?

Financial concern is a major issue for kinship carers. Many families make private arrangements and therefore do not receive any formal statutory support from local authorities. There is a genuine fear that if they ask for help the children will be taken away and as a result, families bear the burden themselves. In many cases families are not aware of the support options available to them or who to turn to for advice. In addition, large numbers of the prisoners are held in custody but on remand, which makes it difficult for families to plan ahead, leaving them confronting many uncertainties. Families are reluctant to finalise childcare arrangements as they are hopeful that the remanded parent in prison will be found 'not guilty'. Inconsistency in the level of support across different geographical locations is also a major factor in financial concerns. The level of support is often dependent on where you live. For example, some local authorities have dedicated teams working with kinship carers and will provide some allowances for them, whilst other local authorities give nothing at all. There can be two grandmothers both looking after their grandchildren, both pensioners, but one will receive £100 per week for the grandchildren and the other will receive nothing. The only difference is where they live.

Managing complex relationships is also a major concern. The relationship between the kinship carer and child can sometimes be a difficult one. Sometimes there are differences in the parenting styles which can lead to conflict between the kinship carer and the parent in prison. Children with a parent in prison often find it hard to talk about what they are feeling or to articulate the impact of their parent being absent.

There is a degree of secrecy about imprisonment which means that children are told not to tell anyone, or they are not told the truth about where the absent parent is ('Mummy's working away'; 'Mummy's gone to hospital'). In both cases the children find it difficult to make sense of where the absent parent has gone and what this means for them and in both cases it means that children are prevented from accessing support from peers, extended family or professionals.

This disruption in their care-giving arrangements can lead to children acting-in or acting-out. They may become depressed, emotionally withdrawn and suffer from anxiety. They may be reluctant to speak to their carer or be unable to do so as the carer tries to cope with the situation by excluding the children from any significant decisions. The children may become disruptive which may manifest itself in the school environment as aggressive behaviour towards their peers and teachers.

Kinship carers may also feel reluctant to take the children to visit their parent in prison due to stigma. There is a great deal of stigma attached to having a family member in prison, stigma attached to visiting a prison, and the fear that children might disclose that they are visiting a prison. Images of prisons portrayed by the media do not give them a family-friendly face, which adds to the family's anxiety about visiting. Often kinship carers will blame themselves or the person they are visiting in prison for their predicament: "Is it my fault my daughter is in prison?"; "How can I care for a child when mine turn out this way?"

Dealing with the stigma and shame of having a parent in prison can be a major issue for children. There is also a degree of stigma attached to being raised by someone other than your parent. Children fear being asked by their peers about why they are living with someone other than their parent. Despite the stigma, children raised by kinship carers tend to feel loved and secure, and report high levels of satisfaction. These placements offer more stability than non-related care as there is a high level of commitment. In relation to support however, the children experience similar hardships to children in the care system, but they (and their carers) receive much less support.

Five children and two homes ... "We are doing everything to keep them in the family"

Liz had five children aged between nine months and 17 years. She was sentenced to two years in prison. Her mother had two of the children, one is five and one is nine years old. Her sister had the nine-month-old baby and Liz's 13-year-old. The 17-year-old floated between homes. Liz wanted her mother and her sister to be able to access greater support but because, as a family, they had opted for a private arrangement, social services did not make an offer of support. Financial support was a major concern for both the carers. At present they are only given vouchers to help with transport cost and meals for the children.

The children faced considerable anxiety about being separated from their mother. The nine month old baby found it hard to adjust to the new surroundings and the absence of her mother. This made it difficult for her aunt who was caring for her. Liz was distraught to be away from her children for the first time. The 17 year old was getting into fights and Liz feared for his future. The 13 year old's performance in school deteriorated and her aunt felt bad because she had to focus all her attention on the baby. The five year old had nightmares and started bedwetting. She was very close to her mother and was now very withdrawn. The grandmother suspected that the 9 year old was being bullied in school but he was reluctant to speak up. The children and carers all therefore experienced difficulties coping and manifested multiple symptoms of distress.

A mother cries for her baby ... "I just want my baby".

Doris was sentenced to five years in prison. She had a two month old child who was cared for by her mother and her partner. She was extremely distressed and wanted help to contact her family. Doris wanted to keep her baby with her in the prison, but her family was strongly against the idea.

She decided to leave the baby with her partner and her mother. Her mother blamed Doris's partner for her involvement in the gang activity that led to Doris being convicted. As a result they had a very tense relationship. The baby was finding it difficult to adjust as he was being breast-fed prior to Doris being arrested. Doris's partner did however offer financial support for the baby and he was able to provide the baby's grandmother with some respite.

A mother's fight for justice... "This is the country they were born and this is where they are staying".

Gina had mental health issues and, as a result, she committed an offence which resulted in her being imprisoned for three years. She had two children aged 6 and 13. The children were cared for by her sister. Her sister also has three children aged five, seven and nine. She lived in a two bedroom property with the five children. Gina was granted permanent residency 15 years ago and both her children were born in the United Kingdom. Gina failed, however, to apply for British citizenship. As a result of her offence Gina was told that she would be facing deportation to a country she had not been to in over 20 years.

The children were placed with her sister as a result of a private arrangement and her sister did not therefore receive any formal support. Her sister's immigration status remained unresolved, so she did not have recourse to public funds. This meant that she could not afford to move into larger accommodation so that the children would be more comfortable, and she was not able to claim housing benefit. Gina's sister worked to support the children and the only help she received was in the form of food vouchers. Gina was appealing against the decision to deport her.

What would make things better for these families?

Greater support for extended family members who volunteer to take on the role of caring for a child whose parent is imprisoned would be a welcome shift in policy. They should be given the same support package: financial, counselling for the children, respite care; that would be offered to a non-related approved foster carer. There should be a national allowance for kinship carers to avoid the "postcode lottery" situation. The support should be given based on the needs of the children and not the means of the carer.

I would also like to see more services that support prisoners, their children and their families. More services that can deal with the difficulties of maintaining contact when a parent is in prison. More services that understand the importance of support groups and home work clubs to support grandparents and other kinship carers. There should be services based in prisons and in communities to bridge the gap.

There should be a greater understanding of the effects of imprisonment and how it affects the wider family. Policies need to be put in place to ensure that families are considered when a child's parent is imprisoned, that these families understand the options available to them and that families are supported throughout the placement.

The Kinship Care Support Service is a model of support which has been developed for kinship carers, where the parent is imprisoned. The model has been successful in supporting kinship carers as well as the parent in prison through pioneering services. These services include a monthly support group which gives kinship carers the opportunity to discuss issues and gain professional advice. Kinship carers can feel they have a voice and the stigma is removed as all involved have a family member in prison.

There is also a weekly homework club, which gives children the chance to freely speak about having a parent in prison. The stigma is again removed as every child present is visiting a parent in prison and is cared for by someone other than their parent. There is a Facebook support group for families which benefits those who find it difficult to visit the prison. There is a dedicated worker who can act as a bridge between kinship carers and the parent in prison. This breaks down the barriers to communicating with a family member in prison.

A policy shift is needed and best practice like this model can lead to better ways of supporting prisoners and their children in the community. The end result would mean prisoners are more settled as they are not worrying about their children. The kinship carers feel supported although they are taking on a huge undertaking.

The workshop at the SRF Conference was well received by the delegates. We were able to explore the difficulties children and families face when a parent is imprisoned and the lack of support available for the children and families of prisoners. We also explored the issues surrounding mother and baby in prison and the impact the environment has on the children. Events like these help to raise awareness of the issues relating to Kinship caring and imprisonment and also to highlight gaps in the support available and give families a voice.

Reference
Women in Prison Prison Reform Trust (2010), London

7. Conference workshop notes

Explaining the prisoner's journey
Lucy Keenan and Chrissie Wild

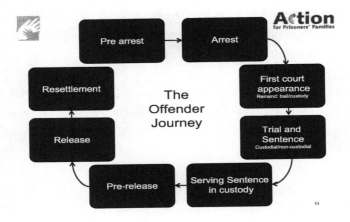

Pre-arrest
The family may be stressed and the individual may be expecting the arrest. There may be unease within the family environment.

Arrest
This may happen early in the morning so as to ensure the alleged offender is in the home. Who sees this arrest? Are children present? Do they see their daddy being taken away in handcuffs? What is explained to them? Children react differently according to age and circumstance.

78

First court appearance

This is when an alleged offender is bailed or remanded in prison. The defendant maybe unexpectedly remanded. Are they the primary carer?

If so arrangements will have to be made for the children? What if they are of school age and are expecting the defendant to pick them up from school? In this case there is nothing put in place for the children.

Trial and Sentence

Stress on the trial impacts on the family. If present at court they hear what their family member is alleged to have done. What are they feeling? This is particularly difficult if a violent or sex offence. There is usually no support for the family at court, only for the witnesses. The case may have been in the press so the family may be known locally.

Serving a sentence

If the defendant is found guilty and sent to prison, where will he/she go? Most prisoners are placed more than 55 miles away from their families. How do families visit? What is it like for children to see a parent locked up and to visit them in an alien environment? How do the families deal with a long period of separation? The effect on children can be devastating.

Pre-release

When a prisoner is coming up to release, the family are not involved in preparations. How do they feel about their family member being released after the time away? A prisoner is prepared for release; the family is not.

Release
When a prisoner comes home (sometimes they may go to a hostel) lots of things may have changed. Children will have got bigger and may have grown up. The ex-prisoner will not be used to the physical environment. The balance of power in the home will have usually shifted.

Resettlement
Does the former prisoner come out of prison to a job? Usually not. The former prisoner and whole family will need to adjust to being together again.

Support for prisoners' families
There is support for the Families of Prisoners but this is patchy. One group that provides comprehensive support is Prisoners' Families and Friends Service (PFFS).
PFFS has teams of volunteers in most of the London Crown Courts and some London Magistrates' Courts, making contact with the families and friends of those sentenced to custody. They also have a family centre which is open two days a week for those whose family member is soon to be, or has been, released from prison. PFFS offer home visits to families of prisoners in the London area who feel alone and need someone to talk to and offers a free phone helpline for those who want telephone support. Their helpline number is 0808 808 3444 and their website is www.pffs.org.uk

Precursors to problems of attachment for young people prior to imprisonment

Demetris Hapeshi and Anthony Sobers

It is widely understood that 'looked after' children are over-represented in the prison population (HM Inspectorate of Prisons, 2011). In its thematic report, HM Inspectorate of Prisons, "The care of looked after children in custody" (2011), estimated that over 25 per cent of those surveyed in young offender institutions reported that they had been in care and this over-representation is repeated in the adult prison population. The publication referred to above, did not breakdown the ethnicity or gender of those surveyed.

The workshop aims were to identify the important building blocks of attachment related to the above in the context of:
1) Relationships
2) Societal perspectives and
3) Communication

The workshop invited:
(a) Small groups or pairs to choose two of the three building blocks (above) and consider these in the light of:
i. The positive and negatives merits of these as they relate to the development of attachment for young people.
ii. The theme of attachment prior to being looked after in a residential facility for children and young people.
iii. The impact of problematic attachment for young people and adults in youth offending and prison situations.

(b) Each group or pair was invited to identify and explore two aspects of help/support they might offer to individuals beset with problems of little or no familial contact and problematic attachment by considering the following:

1. The practitioners' understanding and perspective of problematic attachment behaviours;
2. The personal life experiences of the worker with regard to attachment and problematic attachment behaviours and
3. In the light of the overall context of present day social work practice, how can meaningful help/support be offered to the service user?

c) Each group or pair was invited to select and feedback two aspects developed from the exercise and to link this feedback to either the service user's or practitioner's experience.

In developing our workshop we were mindful of the interesting but perplexing ideas of how to codify and make sense of the problems of attachment for young black and ethnic minority people prior to their custodial experiences. In exploring this through the currently available research material, the identification of black and ethnic minority young people became the initial hurdle insofar as the dimension of race is rarely considered in official statistics relating to custodial sentences. This led to our having to extrapolate from a contextual perspective the number of young adult black and ethnic minority people in custody. A second problem was to recognize that any contextualization of the situation of young black and ethnic minority people coming through the "care system" should not become a negative reinforcement of racist elements identifiable in UK institutions and society at large. But this area of exploration proved to be a dilemma of the first order in that one cannot consider these issues (i.e. attachment, looked after children and custodial sentence figures) without relating these to race. The third issue that we consider was the political and structural issues of policy regarding care and custodial sentencing for black young people.

Workshop findings/issues:

Identification with young people
A number of groups within the workshop identified and discussed their experience of identification/over-identification with young black people. These experiences were often combinations of projections from colleagues as well as their own introjections and identifications. This issue was linked to, but separate from, the issue we have identified (below) as that of "non-conducive environments". The latter includes policy and procedural discourses, whilst the issue of identification/over-identification, we believe, involved less structural and more inter-personal issues.

Non-conducive environments
Inter and intra-professional relations and prescribe Eurocentric "professional boundaries" often prevented black

professionals from having open and frank discussions about the family life and the life experiences of young black people because of entrenched discriminatory notions held about black families and young black people and also discourage (through fear of being branded as not objective or professional enough) meaningful engagement designed to help young black people develop positive attachment experiences.

Working with fathers
Paul Rhys -Taylor and Emmanuel King

You can't unscramble an egg
- Dealing with regret
- Faith helps
- Raising esteem
- Focus on the family

Indirect contact (letters and phone calls)
- Avoiding negative communication
- Anger management tips (James 1:9)
- Being constructive not destructive
- Planning the content of the phone call
- Starting and ending with affirmation
- Careful with the tone of letters
- Get a second opinion before sending

Direct contact (visits)
- Managing communication during visits
- Managing expectations
- Suspicion (encouraging trust)
- Refrain from asking too many questions
- Motive check
- Challenging values and beliefs

Fathering from afar
- Emphasising the importance of fatherhood
- Fathering against all odds (scriptural help)

- Supporting the 'present' parent
- Reasoning with the children (age-appropriate honesty)

Forgiving fathers
- Unforgiving side effects
- Reasons to forgive
- Exercise in forgiveness / prayer
- Grace to you and others going forward

So can you really be a good dad in prison?
"Yes you can be a good dad but you have to really want to carry on."
(Lee – serving four years)
"I'm not as good a dad as I want to be, but you can't give up!"
(Trevor – serving seven years)
"In my opinion the key to being an effective 'prison father' is without doubt communication. What's important is not just the quantity – how many visits or phone calls you can have – but the quality. I find you must be prepared to listen to what they have to say no matter how trivial... Take what joy you can from being with your children for the little time you are given on visits."
(Chris – serving 10 years)
"I feel like I've let my kids down but I'm doing my best to become a better dad and person while I'm in prison. Please God!"
(Mark – serving 12 months)

"Just because we're not there in body does not mean we have to give up. Always remember we can love from a distance. I have met many prisoners who feel that they should give up and go to sleep and never wake up, but when you start to think about your children there is always a good memory to look back on and things don't look as dark. Keep on hoping."

(Wayne – serving eight years)

Appendix: Information for prisoners, people leaving prison and prisoners families

Our thanks to Cherecee Williams, Pact's Kinship Care Support Service Manager for providing this information

These are **some** of the organisations who could help around the general support required:

Pact Kinship Care Support Service
Aims:
• to support family members and friends who care for children whose parents are in HMP Holloway
• to help resolve conflicts between the carers and parents of the children
• to help facilitate contact between children and their parents in these prisons

What does Pact offer?
The Kinship Care Support Service offers a range of support to carers:
• someone to talk to about any concerns you have as a carer
• help to explore how these concerns could be resolved
• relationship counselling for prisoners and kinship carers. This service is offered in partnership with the Marriage Care website and is suitable for all manner of family relationships, not just married couples or partners
• links to a wide range of local and national services
Please contact Cherecee Williams, the Kinship Care Support Service Manager:
Email: cherecee.williams@prisonadvice.org.uk
Tel: 020 7700 1567

Family Rights Group

Family Rights Group provides free, independent advice to parents and other family members whose children are involved with or require social care services from the local authority. They help many families to argue for support services to be provided by the local authority, in particular relatives or friends who take on the care of children when their parents cannot care for them.

They run a telephone and email advice service and have a number of detailed, downloadable advice sheets on all aspects of child care law and practice, which cover topics such as:

- how to apply for a residence order or a special guardianship order without a solicitor and
- the financial impact of a child coming to live with you.

Contact Family Rights Group Advice Service:
Email: advice@frg.org.uk
Phone the advice line: 0808 801 0366, opening hours: Monday to Friday 10am to 3.30pm
Visit www.frg.org.uk/advice_sheets.html for free downloadable advice sheets on all aspects of local authority services for children and families.
Write to them at: Family Rights Group, Second Floor, The Print House, 18 Ashwin Street, London, E8 3DL
Tel: 020 7923 2628
Fax: 020 7923 2683
Email: office@frg.org.uk

Grandparents Association

The Grandparents' Association is committed to supporting and promoting the role, contribution and value of grandparents by:

- Listening to and respecting grandparents

- Providing information, advice and support services which are developed and delivered on the basis of their needs and experiences
- Working with others to advance the profile and status of grandparents
- Promoting awareness of grandparents and grandparenting.

The Grandparents' Association
Moot House, The Stow, Harlow, Essex CM20 3AG
Office: 01279 428040
Helpline: 0845 4349585
Welfare Benefits: 0844 3571033
Email: info@grandparents-association.org.uk

Grandparents Plus
Grandparents Plus is the national charity which champions the vital role of grandparents and the wider family in children's lives - especially when they take on the caring role in difficult family circumstances. They work to support grandparents and the wider family by:
- Campaigning for change so that their contribution to children's wellbeing and care is valued and understood
- Providing evidence, policy solutions and training so that they get the services and support they need to help children thrive
- Building alliances and networks so that they can have a voice and support each other, especially when they become children's full-time carers.

Grandparents Plus
18 Victoria Park Square, Bethnal Green, London E2 9PF
Telephone: 020 8981 8001
Email: info@grandparentsplus.org.uk

The Children's Legal Centre

The Children's Legal Centre is a unique, independent national charity concerned with law and policy affecting children and young people.

It is staffed by lawyers and professionals and has many years of experience in providing legal advice and representation to children, their carers and professionals throughout the UK.

The Children's Legal Centre provides advice on

- Education Law
- Child Law
- Family Law
- Migrant Children's Project
- Publications, consultancy and training
- Research
- International Programmes (The International Section also hosts the Children and Armed Conflict Unit – a joint project with the Human Rights Centre, University of Essex)

The Child Law Advice Line at the Children's Legal Centre

The Child Law Advice Line provides free legal advice and information covering all aspects of law and policy affecting children. An advisor can be contacted on 08088-020-008. The advice line is open from 9.00am to 5.00pm Monday to Friday.

The majority of calls relate to private family law, such as parental responsibility, contact and residence disputes. Other regular subject matters include abduction, adoption, abuse, benefits, child employment, confidentiality, health, housing, maintenance and public proceedings.

Please note that the Child Law Advice Line does not provide advice on criminal offences or juvenile justice.

Action for Prisoners' Families

Action for Prisoners' Families is a membership organisation for those interested in the well being of prisoners' families. It works across sectors: education, health, social care, criminal justice, parenting, etc. to reduce the negative impact of imprisonment.

They represent the views and experiences of their members – organisations providing direct services to the families of people in prison – as well as of families themselves. They support the development of new and existing services, promote good practice on working with prisoners, their children and families both in prison and in the community, publish information, influence policy and raise awareness of the impact of imprisonment on children and families.

The Prisoners' Families Helpline 0808 808 2003 is a free and confidential service for anyone who is affected by the imprisonment of a close family member or friend. It takes over 14,000 calls a year and provides an email and website service for those who would prefer not to use the phone

The Helpline is now open from: 9.00am to 5.00pm Monday to Friday, 10.00am to 3.00pm Saturday. If English is not your first language, the Helpline has access to over 100 languages via language line.

London Head office: Unit 21, Carlson Court, 116 Putney Bridge Road, London, SW15 2NQ
Tel: 020 8812 3600. Fax: 020 8871 0473
E-mail: info@actionpf.org.uk

Sure Start Children's Centres

Children's centres bring together all the different support agencies to offer a wide range of services to meet you and your child's needs, all in one place.

They are somewhere your child can make friends and learn as they play. You can get professional advice on health and family matters, learn about training and job opportunities or just socialise with other people.

There is a wide network of children's centres in England. Finding your local children's centre: You can locate your nearest Sure Start Children's Centre by contacting your local Family Information Service on 08002 346 346.

Family Mediation Helpline

The Family Mediation Helpline is staffed by specially trained operators who provide:
- general information on family mediation;
- advice on whether your case may be suitable for mediation;
- information about eligibility for public funding, and;
- Contact details for mediation services in your local area.

Contact:
Tel: 0845 60 26 627
Email: info@familymediationhelpline.co.uk

Local authority children services department

The level of support you may receive from the local authority is dependent on the needs of the child, the type of arrangement you have to care for the child and the legal status of a child. You can get further advice about this from Family Rights Group (see above)

Women in Prison

3b Aberdeen Studios, 22 Highbury Grove, London N5 2EA
Tel: 020 7226 5879
Website: www.womeninprison.org.uk

WIP has worked to support and advocate for women offenders in prison and on their release and is committed to effecting change within the women's prison system.

Storybook Dads

Every year in the UK, over 160,000 children suffer the trauma of the imprisonment of a parent. We help to maintain the vital emotional bond between parent and child by enabling parents to record bedtime stories onto CD and DVD. Prisoners who maintain contact with their families are up to 6 times less likely to reoffend. Visit: www.storybookdads.org.uk
The group also works in prisons as Storybook Mums.

Prison TalkUk

Is a free forum for anyone with someone in prison or facing prison. Visit www.prisontalkuk.com

Other organisations:

Adfam

Tel: 020 7553 7640
Web: www.adfam.org.uk
Adfam is a national organisation working with and for families affected by drugs and alcohol. They provide direct support to families through publications, training, prison visitors centres, outreach work and signposting to local support services.

Ormiston Children & Families Trust

Central Office, 333 Felixstowe Road, Ipswich, Suffolk, IP3 9BU
Tel: 01473 724517
Provides support services to children and families through more than 20 community and prison based projects.

Law Centres Federation

The LCF is the national body for a network of community based Law Centres. Law Centres provide an independent legal advice and representation service. They employ specialists in areas of 'social welfare' law and help individuals and local groups with problems. To find your local Law Centre, please call 020 7387 8570 or visit the following website www.lawcentres.org.uk

UNLOCK
(The National Association of Reformed Offenders)

Tel: 01634 247 350

Web: http://unlock.org.uk

UNLOCK supports ex-offenders and serving prisoners to overcome social and financial exclusion, plan for life after release and rebuild their lives after leaving crime behind. It provides this support to break the cycle of re-offending and benefit society as a whole.

FPWP/Hibiscus

12 Angel's Gate, 320, City Road, London EC1V 2PI

Tel: 0207 329 2384

Charity that advocates the rights of foreign nationals in UK prisons. FPWP is the Female Prisoners Welfare Project.

NACRO

169 Clapham Road, London SW9 0PU

Tel: 020 7582 6500

Website: www.nacro.org.uk

Since 1966 NACRO has worked to give former offenders, disadvantaged people and deprived communities the help needed to build a better future.

SOVA

1st Floor, Chichester House, 37 Brixton Road, London SW9 6DZ
Tel: 020 7793 0404
Website: www.sova.org.uk
SOVA's mission is to increase the effective involvement of local communities in crime reduction, rehabilitation of offenders and community safety.

Prison Reform Trust

The Prison Reform Trust (PRT) is an independent UK charity working to create a just, humane and effective penal system. We do this by inquiring into the workings of the system; informing prisoners, staff and the wider public; and by influencing Parliament, government and officials towards reform.
The Prison Reform Trust's main objectives are:
1. reducing unnecessary imprisonment and promoting community solutions to crime;
2. improving treatment and conditions for prisoners and their families;
3. promoting equality and human rights in the justice system.
For more information visit: www.prisonreformtrust.org.uk

N.B. There are many other organisations working with prisoners or on prison conditions. Some only cover a small geographical area and therefore have not been included in this section of the book, which does not in any way claim to be comprehensive.

Training Link

Founded in 1985 as Women's Training Link

54-56 Phoenix Road, London NW1 1ES. Tel: 020-7383-5405. Fax: 0871-971-2099.
Email: director@traininglink.org.uk Website: www.traininglink.org.uk
Charity number: 1051662. Company number: 03142188

Training Link is a basic skills training centre based in Somers Town, near Euston and St Pancras stations. We are mainly funded by the Big Lottery Fund and the London Borough of Camden.

The courses we offer include Business Administration, Adult Literacy, English as a Second or Other Language (ESOL), various computer courses and short employment-skills courses, including Food Safety & Hygiene, Customer Care and an Introduction to First Aid. These courses are free for unemployed or people on a low income.

We also offer the European Computer Driving Licence (ECDL) through online distance learning. The full course (7 modules) costs £210, the Flexi-qualification (5 modules) is £150. We are registered with the British Computer Society. Many employers will pay for their staff to do this course.

Our training centre can be hired for meetings in the evenings and at weekends at reasonable rates. We are near Euston and St Pancras-King's Cross stations.

To make a donation to support our work, or find out more about us, visit www.traininglink.org.uk

LOTTERY FUNDED

97

For great rugby league
and sports books, visit

London League Publications
Ltd website:

www.llpshop.co.uk

Biographies of great players and coaches, and club histories.